Little Visits for Families

Little Visits Library

Little
Visits®
for
Families

Little Visits® Library Volume 5

Allan Hart Jahsmann and Martin P. Simon
Illustrated by Hal Lund

CPH.
SAINT LOUIS

Contents

Foreword

Our child Judy loves *Little Visits with God,* and reads her own choices from the book regularly. No single volume has meant as much to our family life as this one.

I have carried the book to Sunday school association meetings, and I have seen eyes light up at the mention of it. My wife has used *Little Visits* to open the day at our church's vacation Bible school. And the children there were glad to listen.

Our own personal experience with these devotions has been multiplied thousands of times in Christian homes throughout our land. The widespread reception given the first volume of this type of material is largely because of the word-of-mouth advertising of grateful readers.

The authors wanted to produce a book that would bring our children (and all of us, I hope, have a lot of child in us) into a face-to-face encounter with the Gospel of Jesus Christ. That they succeeded in doing this with the first *Little Visits* is unquestionable.

The same can be said for this second heartwarming book—and more! Through it all our children will grow happier and stronger in the sunshine of God's love.

Walter Riess

Little Visits® for Families

God is spirit. John 4:24

Why Terrence Couldn't See God

Christy invited her friend Terrence to go to church with her. "It's God's house," explained Christy. "God talks to us there."

So Terrence went to church with Christy. On the way home, Christy asked, "Terrence, how did you like being in church?"

"I liked it okay," he replied, "but where was God? I never saw Him."

"Oh, He was there all the time," Christy said. "But nobody can see God. He isn't like us."

"Why can't we see Him?" asked Terrence. "If we can't see Him, how do we know He's there?"

"Can you see the wind?" Christy's mother asked.

"No," said Terrence.

"Then how do you know there's a wind?" asked Christy's mother.

"I can see what the wind does in the trees. And I can feel it in my face," Terrence replied.

"Well, God is a spirit. He doesn't have a body," Christy's mother explained. "But we can see what He does. And we can feel Him as He puts His love in our hearts. And we can hear Him speak when we listen to His Word."

"I guess you have to go to church awhile before you can see God that way," said Terrence.

"You don't even have to go to church to see God that way," said Christy. "You can love Him anywhere. But going to church helps you know Him because you learn about Him there."

Let's talk: What did Christy call the church? Why did she call it God's house? What did Terrence say on the way home? Why didn't Terrence see God? In what ways is the wind like God? Memorize the Bible verse.

Older children and adults may read: John 4:19–24

Let's pray: Dear God, our Father in heaven, we're glad that You are a spirit so You can be in all places. We know You are in our church, in our homes, and in our hearts. Continue to live with us in our hearts and homes. We ask this through Jesus Christ, our Lord. Amen.

I meditate on [God's Word] all day long. Psalm 119:97

What's in Your Bible?

"Most people don't know what's in the Bible," said the minister as he visited at Shannon's home.

"I know what's in the Bible," said Shannon.

"You do?" asked the minister. "What's in the Bible, Shannon?"

"Mommy's ticket for a turkey, and one of my baby curls, and a dried-up flower. That's what's in the Bible," she responded proudly.

Do you think Shannon knew what's in the Bible? No, she only knew some *things* that her mother had put in the Bible. Shannon didn't know that God's Word is in the Bible and that the way to life with God is in the Bible.

We can't find out what's in the Bible just by owning the book and putting things into it. God's Word has to be learned, and a person has to think about what it says.

Long ago a man who loved God said, "I think about God's Word all day long." Do we think about what God has told us in the Bible every day? all day long? at different times of the day?

To be able to think about God's Word by ourselves, we have to know what it says. That's why we need to read and study the Bible and think about God's Word every day. Memorizing Bible verses helps us think about God's Word.

Even if you're too young to read, you can ask someone to read you a Bible story every day. You can ask someone to teach you a Bible verse. If you're learning how to read, but you can't read the Bible yet, read a Bible storybook or a children's devotion book. Think about what the books say about the Bible.

If you can read the Bible by yourself, do it every day. Then you'll learn what's in the Bible. You'll learn that God hates and punishes sin, but He sent His Son, Jesus, to be our Savior. You'll learn that Jesus died on the cross and rose again so that we can have God's forgiveness. And you'll learn how to live with God as one of His children.

Such things are worth thinking about every day.

Let's talk: What did Shannon say was in the Bible? What did the minister mean when he said, "Most people don't know what's in the Bible"? How can young children find out what's in the Bible? What have you learned from the Bible? Why is it good to think about God's Word all day long?

Older children and adults may read: Psalm 119:97–105

Let's pray: Forgive us, heavenly Father, for knowing so little about what You have told us in the Bible. Teach us to be daily Bible readers, and give us the Holy Spirit so that we will gladly think about Your Word all day long, every day. We ask this in Jesus' name. Amen.

If God is for us, who can be against us? Romans 8:31

God on Our Side

"You can't go along to the picnic," Thomas told his youngest sister. "You're too little. You'll have to stay home."

Thomas was only teasing her, but Cecily started to cry. Then she ran to her father. "Thomas says I'm too little to go on the picnic," Cecily sobbed.

"Well, you tell Thomas he doesn't get to decide who goes along and who doesn't. I decide, and I want you to go," said Father.

Cecily was all smiles again. She didn't care if Thomas was against her—her father was for her. "Daddy's on my side, and he said I could go, and you can't stop me," Cecily told her big brother.

The apostle Paul used some words almost like Cecily's to describe God, our Father in heaven. Paul said, "If God is for us, who can be against us?"

Sometimes people are against us. They don't love us and may even try to hurt us. And worse than that, the devil is against us. He constantly tempts us to sin and to turn away from God. He wants us to follow him instead of God.

But Jesus died for us. He brought us back to God. That's why the Bible says, "He who did not spare His own

Son, but gave Him up for us all—how will He not also ... graciously give us all things?"

If God loves us so much that He gave up His only Son's life, then He is for us. And if God is for us, who can be against us? Nobody, not even the devil. We can say, "Go away, devil. Jesus paid for my sins. You can't say that I won't get into heaven."

That's why Paul also wrote, "Nothing will be able to separate us from the love of God that's in Christ Jesus our Lord."

Let's talk: Why did Cecily cry? What made her smile? Who is against us? Why can we be sure that God is for us? What is the answer to the question "If God is for us, who can be against us?" Where will all who believe in Jesus get to go even if the devil says they can't?

Older children and adults may read: Romans 8:31–39

Let's pray: Dear Jesus, we love You for what You did for us. Because You died for us, God is on our side. If God is for us, who can be against us? Help us believe that nothing can separate us from the love of God that we have because of You. Keep us happy in Your love. Amen.

Delight yourself in the LORD and He will give you the desires of your heart. Psalm 37:4

How to Be Happy

"I never get what I want," said Emilio.

"I know how to change that," said his brother, Nicolaus. "Start wanting what you get!"

At first Emilio thought his brother was just making fun of him. But then he thought about it. "Maybe the things I get are what God wants me to have," he said. "Maybe it wouldn't be good to get everything I want. Maybe when I pray for something, I should ask God to give me what's best for me."

"I know a Bible verse that tells you how to get what you want," Nicolaus said. He picked up the Bible from the table and showed Emilio Psalm 37:4. "See, the psalm writer said, 'Delight yourself in the LORD and He will give you the desires of your heart.'"

We can learn to like almost anything. Some people like olives, others don't. Some like company, others would rather be alone. Some like to read, others would rather play ball or go fishing.

We usually like what we learn to like. So why not learn to like what God likes? That's the way to become satisfied and happy. When we love God and the things He likes, we trust that He will give us what we want and need.

Let's talk: Why did Emilio complain a lot? What did Nicolaus tell him? When does the Lord give us what we want? What are some things that we know God wants us to have? How do we learn to love the Lord and what He wants?

Older children and adults may read: Psalm 37:1–9

Let's pray: Dear Father in heaven, please give us the Holy Spirit so that we can follow Jesus, our Savior, and enjoy being Your children. Help us love what You love. Help us to be happy with the good things You give us every day. In Jesus' name. Amen.

I am troubled by my sin. Psalm 38:18

Not Easy but Right

"Okay, I admit I shouldn't have done it," said Rasheeda. She had ruined Lucas' picture, and her father was making her tell Lucas she was sorry. But Rasheeda didn't want to.

"That's not being sorry," said Lucas.

"I said I shouldn't have done it, and that's all I'm going to say," Rasheeda snapped.

"Well," said Dad, "God wants us to admit our sins, but just saying 'I did wrong' isn't enough. He also wants us to be sorry."

"All right then, I'm sorry," said Rasheeda, feeling meaner than ever. "What else do you want me to say?"

Her father was sad that Rasheeda felt the way she did. "It's not just the words that count," he said. "Once there was a man who kissed Jesus, and even that was a sin. Do you remember who it was?"

"Judas," said Rasheeda, still pouting.

"Yes, Judas didn't really mean his kiss because he did not love Jesus," explained Dad. "Don't you see? It makes a difference *why* you do something or *why* you say something. A kiss isn't a kiss if there isn't any love with it."

For a minute everybody was quiet. Then Rasheeda said, "I'm sorry I ruined your picture, Lucas. You can have mine instead."

"I don't need yours, Rasheeda. But I'm glad you're really sorry," he said.

It isn't always easy to say "I'm sorry," and it's even harder to *be* sorry. But God wants us to be sorry for what we do wrong. When we aren't sorry, we're telling God, "I don't *want* Your forgiveness. I want to stay bad." How can God forgive us then?

Yet God is always willing to forgive us for Jesus' sake. That's plenty of reason for admitting our sins and being sorry about them.

Let's talk: What had Rasheeda done? What did she say? Why didn't Lucas like what she said? Why wasn't Judas' kiss really a kiss? Why isn't it enough just to say "I'm sorry"? What good reasons do we have for being sorry about our sins?

Older children and adults may read: Luke 15:11–24

Let's pray: O Lord, please make us willing to admit our sins to You and to those whom we have hurt. Most of all, help us to be sorry for our sins. Forgive all our sins for the sake of Jesus, our Savior, who died to pay for them. In His name we pray. Amen.

Give thanks to the LORD, for He is good; His love endures forever. Psalm 118:1

Something That Lasts and Lasts

"That's the third time those kids ran over my flowers," said Mrs. Rather. "That's enough. I'm not going to let them play in my yard anymore."

Mrs. Rather put a lock on the gate to her yard, and the children couldn't play there anymore. They missed playing in her yard because she had a fort with swings and a slide for her grandchildren.

One day two of the kids asked Mrs. Rather if they could play in her yard again. "We promise to be real careful about your flowers," they said.

"No, you had your chance," Mrs. Rather answered. "I told you twice to keep off the flowers." And she didn't open the gate.

We can be glad that God isn't like Mrs. Rather. When we tell God we're sorry for what we've done wrong, does God ever close the gate? No, God always forgives for Jesus' sake. He always wants us near Him.

The Bible says, "God's love endures forever." It never wears out; it never ends. That's something to be glad about. So we say with the psalm writer, "Give thanks to the LORD, for He is good; His love endures forever."

Let's talk: What made Mrs. Rather angry? How long does God's love last? If we ask God to forgive us, will He do it? Will He do it if He already has done it a hundred times? Why is God willing to forgive us? Why does He love us? What does the Bible verse tell us to do?

Older children and adults may read: Psalm 117

Let's pray: For Your love that never ends, we thank You, dear Father in heaven. Please help us live like people who love You. Give us the Holy Spirit so that we will always treat others as we want to be treated. We ask this in Jesus' name. Amen.

The LORD gives sight to the blind. Psalm 146:8

Learning to See Jesus' Way

Julie was talking to a man who was blind. He was telling her about the things he did and the places he liked to go.

"How can you do so many things when you can't see?" Julie asked.

The man reached down and patted his dog. "My dog sees for me," he answered. You could hear how he felt about his dog in the way he said it.

It's wonderful that dogs can be trained to help people who can't see. The dogs use their eyes for those who can't

see. They lead the blind safely across dangerous streets and wherever they want to go.

Jesus often said that some people have eyes but can't see. He meant they can't see their sin. They can't see that their life is dark. They can't see the way to heaven. They can't see the way God wants them to live.

But those who believe in Jesus are led by Him. We get His eyes. He shows us that we sin. He saves us and takes us to heaven. He helps us see what God wants us to do. The Bible says, "The LORD gives sight to the blind."

We can help those who can't see God and His love even though they have good eyes. We can tell them that Jesus is their Savior. We can show what He means to us through the way we talk and act. As the Holy Spirit works in the hearts of those we tell, they begin to see that God loves them.

And how well do *we* see God and His ways? The Lord will open our eyes as He leads us. That's why we pray, "Open our eyes."

Let's talk: What did Julie ask the man who was blind? What did he tell her? What does a seeing-eye dog do for its master? In what way are people blind even though they can see? What does Jesus help us see? How do we help people see that God loves them? Why do we need to ask the Lord to open our eyes?

Older children and adults may read: Acts 26:14–18

Let's pray: Dear Jesus, please open our eyes and keep them open so that we won't be blind about our sins and God's wonderful love. Help us show others that You are their Lord and Savior. Make us all glad to follow You because we know that You are leading us to heaven. Amen.

[God] also made the stars. Genesis 1:16

In the Middle of God's World

Seth and his sister, Jana, sat watching the stars. The paper had said there would be a pretty show of northern lights in the sky that evening.

"You can point to any star," said Seth, "and it's millions and millions of miles away."

"They must be awfully big, or we couldn't see them," said Jana.

"So big we can't even think how big," said Seth.

"You know how big an atom is?" asked Jana. "There are millions of them in one little thimble, that's how small they are." She'd heard this in science class.

"That's funny," said Seth.

"What's funny?" asked Jana.

"I don't mean funny. I mean, well, *wonderful,* I guess," Seth explained. "When you think of the world, you begin to understand how great God is."

"You mean because He made both the atoms and the stars?" asked Jana.

"Yeah. And both at the same time," said Seth. "Stars so very, very big that we can't even imagine how big they are. And atoms so very, very small that we can't even imagine how small they are."

"You know what?" said Jana after thinking a while. "We're in the middle between the great big things and the very little things God created."

Then they both just sat and looked and thought some more. But it was like praying.

Let's talk: How far away are the stars? How big is an atom? What did Seth think was wonderful about it all? Can you tell the Bible story about creation? Where do we find this story in the Bible?

Older children and adults may read: Genesis 1:14–19

Let's pray: O great and mighty God, Maker of the stars, we see how small we are when we think of the great wonders You have made. We wonder why You care about us. But we're glad that You love us and have adopted us as Your children. Forgive our sins for Jesus' sake, and make Your love shine in our lives. In Jesus' name we pray this. Amen.

He who has been stealing must steal no longer.
Ephesians 4:28

Finders Keepers?

On the way to school, Brock saw something that looked like a baseball under a bush in front of a house. When he crawled under the bush, he saw it *was* a baseball. He was happy.

"Finders keepers," he said and took the ball to school. He knew that it probably belonged to the girl who lived in the house where he found it, but he didn't care. He wanted the ball.

That evening Brock took a different way home from school. As he walked down the alley, he heard a dog barking. "That's Patches!" Brock cried.

He went inside the yard and saw the dog he had gotten for his birthday. He thought Patches had run away, but there he was, wiggling all over. Somebody had tied him up, so Brock petted Patches and started to untie him.

"Get away from my dog," said the big boy who lived there. "I found him. Beat it or I'll punch you."

Brock ran home crying. Now he didn't think "finders keepers" was a good rule. He was sorry he ever thought so. He asked Jesus to forgive him for taking the ball.

Brock went to the house where he had found the ball. He saw a girl in the yard, so he stopped. "Is this yours?" he asked. Brock knew that Jesus wanted him to return the ball.

"Yes," said the girl. "Where did you find it?"

"Never mind," said Brock, and he tossed the ball to her. Then he walked on home, muttering to himself.

As he walked down the street, Brock heard a dog yelping behind him. It was Patches. Part of the rope was hanging from his neck.

"Patches!" called Brock, hugging and petting his dog. "You tore yourself loose to come back to me. 'Finders keepers' is sure an awful rule. Now I know why Jesus does not want us to steal."

Let's talk: What did Brock find on his way to school? Why did he keep the ball? What happened on the way home from school? Who said "finders keepers" this time? How did Brock show that he didn't believe the rule anymore? What does God say about stealing? What's our best reason for not stealing?

Older children and adults may read: Ephesians 4:25–30

Let's pray: Dear Father in heaven, please forgive us for wanting things You have given to other people. Help us to be satisfied with what we have and willing to help other people keep what is theirs. We ask this in Jesus' name. Amen.

The LORD smelled the pleasing aroma. Genesis 8:21

The Perfume of Love

Daniel lived near a lake. One day he saw some flowers growing by the water. "How pretty!" Daniel said. "I'll pick some for my mom and dad."

Daniel didn't know that these flowers were called skunk cabbage. They have a bad smell. Most people don't want them in their house.

When Daniel brought the flowers to his mother, she said, "Thank you, Dan. You're very sweet."

But his big sister said, "They smell awful! You aren't going to keep them in the house, are you, Mom?"

"They smell sweet to me because I smell the love of my son in them," Mom answered.

Did Daniel's mother really smell love? Can anyone smell love? Well, not really, but you know what Daniel's mother meant. Even though the smell was bad, she liked the flowers because they told her that Daniel loved her.

Noah burned an offering of thanks to God for saving him and his family from the flood. The Bible says, "The LORD smelled the pleasing aroma." Does God smell offerings or fires? No, not like we do. But He knows the love that goes with the offerings. And He smells our love the way Daniel's mother smelled his love.

In another place the Bible says, "Christ loved us and gave Himself up for us as a fragrant offering and sacrifice to God." Those who follow Jesus want to be like Him and walk in His footsteps of love.

When we love other people for Jesus' sake, "We are to God the aroma of Christ." Does that mean God can smell us? No, not with a nose. But God sees that we love Him, and it's the "aroma" of our love that God smells. Our love is like a sweet perfume to God.

≈

Let's talk: What kind of flowers did Daniel see? Why did he pick them? Why did his mother say, "They smell sweet to me"? Why did God say that Noah's offering smelled sweet to Him? What kind of sweet-smelling offering did Jesus give for us? When do our offerings smell sweet to God?

Older children and adults may read: Genesis 8:18–22

Let's pray: Heavenly Father, we're glad that You love us for Jesus' sake. Even though we sin a lot, may Jesus' love for us and our love for Him make everything we do smell sweet to You. Amen.

You shall not steal. Exodus 20:15

Fair Trading

Melissa was bouncing her new basketball in her driveway. She had just gotten it for her birthday. Jack rode by on his bike. He was older than Melissa and usually didn't pay any attention to her. But when he saw Melissa's new ball, he stopped.

"Hi, Melissa," said Jack. "Where did you get the new basketball?"

"I got it for my birthday," Melissa answered. She was a little surprised that Jack was so friendly.

"That's pretty nice," said Jack. "I've got a new watch. Wanna take a look at it?" asked Jack, holding out his wrist. The watch was only worth about $7.00.

Melissa looked at the watch. "That's real gold," said Jack. "Wouldn't you like a watch like this? Maybe we can make a trade. I'll trade you for your basketball."

"Would you really?" asked Melissa.

"Sure," said Jack.

That evening Jack asked his father to put up a basket for him so he could practice shooting the basketball. "Where'd you get the ball?" Jack's father asked. Jack was

ashamed to tell, but he finally told his father what he had done.

"Do you think that was a fair trade?" Dad asked.

"No," answered Jack. "I guess I cheated Melissa."

"Well, what do you think you should do about it?" asked Dad.

"Guess I'd better take the ball back to her," said Jack.

"That's a good idea, son," said Dad. "And next time be sure you make a fair trade. Cheating is stealing, and you know what God says about stealing."

"I'm sorry," said Jack. "It was a dirty trick."

"Well, God will forgive you. You need to ask Melissa to forgive you too," said Dad.

Let's talk: What does God say about stealing? Why is cheating a sin like stealing? How did Jack cheat Melissa? When is God willing to forgive stealing? Why? What do you think Jesus wants His children to do with things that belong to other people?

31

Older children and adults may read: Acts 9:36–40

Let's pray: Dear Father in heaven, for Jesus' sake forgive us if we have cheated someone or tried to take what wasn't ours. Make us willing to help others keep what belongs to them. In Jesus' name we ask this. Amen.

But the wisdom that comes from heaven is ... peace-loving.
James 3:17

Why Mark Never Got Angry

"Hi there, Lanky-legs," yelled a boy from across the street. He wasn't trying to be mean. He just didn't know how cruel it can be to call other people names they don't like.

But it didn't seem to bother Mark. He just grinned and yelled back, "Lanky-legs will beat you in a race any time."

Mark didn't become angry when anyone called him names. "You can't ever pick a fight with Mark," his parents said.

"How come you're so easy to get along with?" Raphael asked him.

"I learned a secret from my mother," answered Mark. "When I was 4 years old, somebody called me a dog. I cried and wanted my mother to hit him. But my mother said, 'People called Jesus many bad names, and Jesus never hurt them back. You want to be like Him, don't you?'

"Then she taught me a verse from the Bible. It said, 'The wisdom that comes from heaven is ... peace-loving.'

" 'If we're really wise, as wise as God can make us,' she told me, 'then nobody can make us angry or make us argue and fight.' "

People treated Jesus much worse than anyone will ever treat us, and Jesus didn't fight back. He didn't even hate them. He forgave them. Jesus came from heaven to make peace between God and people. Those who have His Spirit try to get along peacefully with one another.

Let's talk: What did someone call Mark? Why didn't he get angry? What secret did he learn from his mother? What Bible verse did his mother teach him? How did Jesus make peace between God and us? How can we become more peace-loving, like Jesus?

Older children and adults may read: James 3:13–17

Let's pray: Dear Jesus, we're glad that You are kind and peace-loving. We're glad that You were willing to be hurt for us. Please make us wise and peace-loving too so that we won't mind when people are mean to us. Help us forgive others as You forgive us. Amen.

God demonstrates His own love for us in this: While we were still sinners, Christ died for us. Romans 5:8

How Good God Is

"You mean God hears everything I say, every word?" Randy asked his Sunday school teacher.

"Not only every word you *say,*" said Mrs. Miller, "but every word you *think.*"

"Like when I'm mad and think I'm going to run away—God hears what I think?" Randy asked.

"Yes, He does," said Mrs. Miller.

"Then I guess God doesn't like me," said Randy. "I think a lot of bad things."

"No," said Mrs. Miller. "That's what's so good about God. He knows how bad we are, but He still loves us. Do you want to learn a Bible verse about that?"

"Sure," said Randy. "I didn't know God was so good."

"Here's one from Romans. Why don't you sit down and copy it? Then you can take it home and memorize it," suggested Mrs. Miller.

While Randy was copying it, the other children looked up Romans 5:8 in their Bibles and started learning it. It wasn't hard to learn. It said, "God demonstrates His own love for us in this: While we were still sinners, Christ died for us."

The children said it, and Randy said it too. Soon everybody knew it.

"I'm glad God loves people even though they're sinners," said Randy. "Otherwise He wouldn't love me."

Let's talk: What bothered Randy? Why did he think God couldn't like him? What did Mrs. Miller tell Randy about God? What Bible verse did Mrs. Miller find for Randy? What does it mean? Why did this verse make Randy happy?

Older children and adults may read: Psalm 139:1–12

Let's pray: Dear heavenly Father, we're glad that You love us even though we're sinners. We thank You for sending Jesus to die for us and save us from our sins. Please forgive the many words we say that aren't good. Help us think good thoughts and say kind words. We ask this in Jesus' name. Amen.

Trust in the LORD. Psalm 37:3

Whistle, Don't Crawl

The weather was very cold, and the ice on the river was frozen all the way to the bottom. A man walked down to the river. He wanted to cross, but there wasn't any bridge. I wonder if this ice will hold me? he thought to himself.

For a long time he looked at the ice. Then he decided it would hold him, but he wasn't sure. "If I crawl across, it won't break as easily," the man told himself. So he crawled across the river on his stomach. The ice held him, but he was worried all the time.

When he got to the other side, the man saw a pickup

truck driving toward the river. Without stopping, the truck drove onto the ice and across the river. A boy was riding in the truck with his father. The boy never worried a bit that the ice would break. In fact, he was whistling a happy song.

Which one was safer on the ice—the happy boy or the scared man? They were both safe. But there was a great difference between them. The boy who trusted his father was safe and happy. The man who didn't trust the ice was safe but worried.

Some Christians are like the boy; others are like the man. Some trust that God will bring them safely to heaven. They're happy with God and don't worry. Others are worried that they will lose their faith or that their faith isn't strong enough. These people crawl when they could ride and whistle.

You have Jesus, your Savior, with you every day. So trust Him. Be happy. Don't worry. Don't crawl. Ask Him to take care of you on your way to heaven. Then trust Him to get you there safely.

The Bible says, "God's power has given us everything we need for life." So do what the psalm writer said, "Trust in the LORD." Then you'll feel like whistling.

Let's talk: How did the man cross the ice? Why? How did the boy cross the ice? Why was the boy whistling? What kind of Christians are like the man who crawled across the ice? Why can we be happy like the boy? What does the Bible verse tell us?

Older children and adults may read: Psalm 91

Let's pray: Thank You, dear Lord, for promising to take care of us on the way to heaven. Please help us trust You so that we will be happy as You lead us home. Amen.

Without [Jesus] nothing was made that has been made.
John 1:3

When Dad Made Fruit Punch

Hanako watched with big eyes. Her dad took a pitcher of clear water, poured something into it from a canister, and suddenly the water was a pretty red. He had made fruit punch. Hanako liked fruit punch.

"Dad, can you make wine out of water the way Jesus did?" Hanako asked.

Dad smiled. "No, Hanako, I couldn't do that. Only Jesus could do that," he answered.

"But you made fruit punch," said Hanako.

"I only added something to the water to make it taste good. Jesus changed the water into wine. That's much different," Dad explained.

"Jesus can do anything, can't He?" asked Hanako.

"Yes, together with God the Father and the Holy Spirit, Jesus created all the water and the air and the land, all the stars, too, and the moon and the sun ..." Dad said.

"... and the trees and Kitzen and me?" asked Hanako.

"Yes," Dad answered. "The Bible says, 'All things were made through Jesus, and without Him nothing was made that has been made.' Most people don't know this. That's why they don't thank Him. Do you think you can remember the Bible verse?"

"Without Jesus nothing was made that has been made," repeated Hanako, and her dad gave her a big glass of fruit punch.

$$\approx$$

Let's talk: What did Hanako's dad make using water? How did he do it? What did Jesus make using water? How did

He do it? What does the Bible say has Jesus made? Whom should we thank for the world and the things in it?

Older children and adults may read: Hebrews 1:1–10

Let's pray: Lord Jesus, we thank You for all the things You have made for our good. We can see Your love for us in what You have made. We can see Your love especially in what You did for us when You died for us. We love You because You first loved us. Help us live as You want us to every day. Amen.

Whatever you do, do it all for the glory of God.
1 Corinthians 10:31

How a Wrong Answer Was Right

A new minister came to Grace Church. The first person he met was the janitor.

"Good morning," the minister said, "I'm the new minister. And what work do you do for the Lord?"

The janitor answered, "I do all my work for the Lord."

At first the minister thought that was a wrong answer. He had expected the janitor to say, "I clean the church" or "I teach Sunday school." But the more the minister thought about it, the more he liked the janitor's answer.

At the supper table, the minister told his wife about his first day. "I think the janitor has the right idea," the minister said. "I'm going to preach a sermon about her answer."

The very next Sunday, the minister preached a sermon about the janitor's answer. Can you guess what the Bible verse was? "Whatever you do, do it all for the glory of God."

That's the way God wants us to live. Because we belong to Him, He wants us to do everything for Him. When we do things for God, we will be happy. When we work for God, we don't really care how long a job takes or how hard it is or whether anyone says our work is good. We're happy to be doing something for God because we love Him.

Let's talk: What did the new minister ask the janitor? What was the janitor's answer? What did the minister think about the answer? What Bible verse did the minister use for his sermon? How can we do everything for the glory of God? What reasons do we have for doing everything for God?

Older children and adults may read: Romans 12:6–13

Let's pray: We're glad, dear heavenly Father, that we don't have to wait to do great things to honor You. We know we can serve You in whatever we do. Please help us live all our life with You and for You out of love for Jesus, our Savior. We ask this in His name. Amen.

Bridle [your] tongue. James 1:26 (RSV)

A Bridle for Your Tongue

Latasha and André were visiting their grandparents who lived on a farm. As they looked around the barn, they found some old harnesses.

"We used to put them on the horses so they could pull wagons and plows," explained Grandpa.

"What's this piece here?" asked André.

"That's the bridle," said Grandpa. "You see, this round piece of steel went into the horse's mouth. It's called the bit. And these leather straps went over the horse's head and ears to hold the bridle up. Lines called reins snap into the rings on both sides of the mouth."

"The reins were used to steer the horse, weren't they?" said Latasha.

"Well, I guess you could call it steering," said Grandpa. "We called it driving. When you pulled the left rein, the horse would go to the left. When you pulled the right rein, he'd go to the right. By pulling both reins back, you could slow the horse up, keep him from running away, or make him stand still. That's how a bridle works."

"Now I see what Miss Adams meant," said Latasha.

"What'd she say?" asked Grandpa.

"She said the Bible tells us to bridle our tongues," Latasha explained.

"That's a good idea," said Grandpa. "That little talking tongue needs a bridle to make it go the right way. And there's nothing more dangerous than a runaway tongue."

"How can I bridle my tongue?" asked André.

"That's easy. Just let Jesus put His 'bit' into your mouth, and let Him tell you what to say or not to say," answered Grandpa. "That's the same as if Jesus were pulling the reins on a bridle for your tongue."

~

Let's talk: What's a bridle? Where did André and Latasha see one? How are bridles used on horses? What does the Bible say we should bridle? Why do our tongues need to be bridled? What did Grandpa say is the best way to bridle our tongues?

Older children and adults may read: James 3:3–10

Let's pray: Dear Father in heaven, we're sorry that our tongues often run away and say bad words. Please forgive the many times we have sinned with our tongues. Bridle our tongues with the love of Jesus and give us the Holy Spirit to help our tongues say what You want us to say. We ask this in the name of Jesus, our Lord and Savior. Amen.

The word of God is living and active. Hebrews 4:12

When God Talks to Our Hearts

Reba was sitting on her mother's lap, listening to a Bible story. It was the story of Samuel. "Before he was born," said Mother, "Samuel's father and mother gave him to the Lord. They wanted him to belong to God."

Reba loved the story. When the story was over, Reba asked, "Mother, you gave me to God before I was born, didn't you?"

Her mother blushed. "No," she said, "I'm afraid I did not."

Reba felt like crying, but then she got an idea. "Can't you still do it, Mother? Can't you do it *now?*" she asked.

"Yes, I can, and I've done it many times since you were born," Mother answered.

Then she took Reba's hands in hers. "I want you to be God's girl," Mother said. "I want you to belong to Him all your life." Then Reba was happy again.

It wasn't just a Bible story Reba heard. She heard God talking to her through the story. She thought it was wonderful that Samuel was given to God. She wanted that wonderful thing to happen to her.

Our Bible verse says, "The word of God is living and active." Through His Word, God talks to us and the Holy Spirit comes to us. When we listen to God talk to us through Bible stories and verses, something happens to us. God comes into our hearts and leads us to love Him. That's what happened to Reba.

God comes into our hearts especially when we hear about Jesus and His love. When we learn how Jesus died to save us from our sins, then we become sorry for our sins, and we want Him to save us and to change us. And He does.

⌒

Let's talk: What Bible story did Reba hear? What did Reba ask her mother? How did Reba's mother give her to God? What did Reba hear besides just a Bible story? How does God talk to us? What happens when God talks to us and we hear Him?

Older children and adults may read: 1 Samuel 1:21–28

Let's pray: Dear Father in heaven, we're glad that we are Your children. Whenever we hear Your Word, help us hear more than just the words. Come into our hearts and change us for Jesus' sake. Amen.

Sing to the LORD. Psalm 96:2

Nickels for Rats

When Charles Spurgeon was a boy, he lived in a place where there were many rats. His mother hated rats. She also wanted her son to learn hymns. So Charles' mother paid him a nickel for every rat he killed and a nickel for every hymn he learned.

How would you like to get a nickel for every hymn you learn? Would you learn more hymns if you got a dollar for each one? Spurgeon later became a great preacher. He said he made more money killing rats than learning hymns, but the hymns did him much more good.

Next time you're in trouble or scared, try singing a hymn. Next time you feel hurt or alone, sing a hymn. Instead of worrying, sing a hymn. Hymns help to keep God in your heart.

When you sing hymns, sing them to the Lord. The psalm verse says, "Sing to the LORD." Another psalm says, "Make a joyful noise to the LORD." Your singing doesn't have to be good. Maybe other people will call it noise, but God will be glad when you sing to Him.

We have lots of reasons for singing to God. He sent Jesus to save us by dying for us. He loves us. Jesus has made us God's children. "Sing to the LORD." Knowing hymns helps us do that.

⌒

Let's talk: For what did Charles Spurgeon's mother give him nickels? What are some better reasons for learning hymns? What hymns can you sing without a book? What does the psalm verse say? What are some reasons for singing to the Lord?

Older children and adults may read: Psalm 96

Let's pray: Lord God, we thank You for the people who have written good hymns for us to sing. You have given us many reasons for singing to You. Give us the Holy Spirit so that we will want to learn hymns and make a joyful noise by singing to You. Amen.

Come, Lord Jesus. Revelation 22:20

When He Comes

Miranda was standing with her nose pressed against the window. It was after 5 p.m. It was almost time for Dad to come home from work. Miranda loved her dad a lot and often stood by the window so she could see him come home.

"Mom, what time is it? Isn't it time for Dad to be here?" Miranda asked. "I wish he'd come."

When Miranda's dad pulled into the driveway, she ran out to meet him. He took her in his arms and carried her into the house. Miranda was happy—her dad had come home.

Did you know that we are waiting for someone? Somebody special? He's been away a long time, but we're sure that He's coming back. We're waiting for Jesus. Before Jesus went back to heaven, He promised that He would come again.

When Jesus comes, He will take us all to heaven to be with Him. That's why we're so happy that He's coming. We can be just like Miranda who couldn't wait for her dad to come home.

Let's talk: Why did Miranda wait for her dad to come home? How did she feel when he arrived? For whom are all of God's children waiting? Why will we be happy when

Jesus comes again? What prayer does our Bible verse teach us to say?

Older children and adults may read: Revelation 22:12–17

Let's pray: Dear Lord, we're glad that You are coming again. Come, Lord Jesus, and take us to heaven. Amen.

If we confess our sins, [God] ... will forgive us our sins.
1 John 1:9

When Hernando Confessed

Hernando had just come back from the grocery store. "Put the change in my purse, please," said his mother.

"Sure, Mom," said Hernando. When he found his mother's purse, he began putting the change into it. He noticed quite a few coins already in the purse.

Mom will never know if I keep a couple quarters,

Hernando thought. Besides, I deserve some money for going to the store, he told himself. So Hernando kept 75 cents for himself.

When Hernando came into the kitchen, his mother said, "Thanks for going to the store for me. I know you're saving to get a new baseball, so you can have a dollar for helping me."

Now Hernando felt ashamed of what he had done. "Mom," he said, "I already took 75 cents. I know I should not have. I know it was stealing. I'm sorry I did it. Please forgive me."

"I'm glad you know it was wrong to take the money," Mom said. "I'm also glad you admitted what you did. Of course I'll forgive you. Every day I do things I shouldn't do. So I ask God to forgive me just as you asked me to forgive you. And He always does."

"I'm glad you and God love me so much that you both forgive me," said Hernando. Then he gave his mother a big hug and went and put the quarters back in her purse.

⌒

Let's talk: What sin did Hernando do when he put his mother's change away? Why was he sorry for what he had done? How did he confess his sin? Why was Hernando's mother willing to forgive him? What does the Bible say about God's forgiveness? Why did Hernando put the money back in his mother's purse?

Older children and adults may read: Psalm 51:1–12

Let's pray: Lord God, our Father in heaven, how glad we are that You are always willing to forgive our sins for Jesus' sake! Teach us to confess our sins every day so that we may enjoy Your love and forgiveness. In Jesus' name we ask this. Amen.

Everyone who loves ... knows God. Whoever does not love does not know God, because God is love. 1 John 4:7–8

Getting to Know God

Neil's parents got a divorce and put him in a foster home. He thought no one cared about him, so he ran away twice. Each time he ran away, Neil got caught stealing food. When the police took him back to the foster home, Neil hated everybody.

One day a couple came to adopt Neil. Mr. and Mrs. Lea took Neil to their home with them. They said if he liked them and they liked him, they would adopt him. But Neil said to himself, They don't love me, and I don't love them. I'll do what they tell me to, but I'm not going to let them fool me.

The Leas tried to love Neil. They did everything they could for him. And Neil did what he was told to do, but he never smiled. He never said "Thank you" or "I love you." He never felt as though he belonged. Neil felt like a stranger in their house.

Finally, Mr. Lea told his wife, "I'm afraid we'll have to give Neil up. We just can't win his heart."

That same day, Neil broke his leg. Mrs. Lea took him to the hospital. She stayed with him as they set the leg and put on the cast. Then for weeks after he came home, Mr. Lea carried Neil up and down steps and around the house.

One day as he was being carried, Neil hugged Mr. Lea for being so good to him. Then Neil started to cry. He told the Leas he wanted to stay with them and be their son.

Neil didn't really know how much Mr. and Mrs. Lea loved him until he began to love them. And he didn't enjoy their love and feel at home with them until he believed that they loved him. But how different everything seemed when he wanted to belong to them.

Without love, we can't feel at home with God either. Just doing some things God wants us to do won't make us His children. It won't even help us to know God.

But when we see and believe that He loves us, then we love Him and try to please Him. The Bible says, "Everyone who loves ... knows God. Whoever does not love does not know God, because God is love."

Let's talk: Why was Neil unhappy at the foster home? What did Mr. and Mrs. Lea offer to do for Neil? Why did they think they would have to give him up? What changed Neil and made him want to belong to the Lea family? Who makes us feel close to God? How can we be sure that God loves us?

Older children and adults may read: 1 John 4:7–12

Let's pray: We don't only want to obey You, dear God, we want to enjoy *belonging* to You. Please help us understand how good You really are so that we will always love You and want to be Your children forever. We ask this through Jesus Christ, our Lord. Amen.

Do not let any [bad] talk come out of your mouths, but only what is helpful. Ephesians 4:29

Afraid of a Little Lettuce

There was a big family dinner at the Smith house. The dining room table was too small. Two other tables were set up. The three tables stretched from the dining room through the living room.

Aunt Emily was at one end of the table, and Jacob was at the other end. Jacob looked at Aunt Emily and smiled. Then he looked at her salad. It was half of a peach on some lettuce. A little piece of lettuce was on the peach, but Jacob couldn't see what it really was.

"Aunt Emily, is that a worm on your peach?" he asked.

Jacob didn't mean to say anything bad. But Aunt Emily couldn't eat her peach after that. She knew the little green thing was only a sliver of lettuce, but now she couldn't eat it. She kept thinking about the worm Jacob had said it might be.

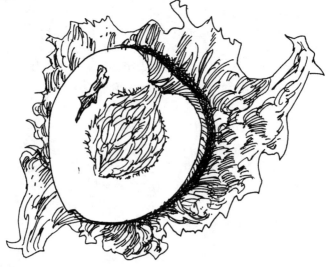

That's how strong words are. Jacob didn't tie Aunt Emily up or hold back her arm. He just talked. But his words kept her from eating.

Words are often more powerful than we think. They can do a lot to people. They can do good, and they can do harm. That's why the Bible tells us to be careful with how we talk. In Ephesians 4, God says, "Do not let any [bad] talk come out of your mouths, but only what is helpful."

Good words help other people. And the best words tell

others about God's love. Do you know what kind of talk that is? It's talk about Jesus and what He did for us.

Let's talk: Why couldn't Aunt Emily eat her peach? What else can words do to people? What kind of words are bad? What kind of talking does the Bible verse tell us to do? When are our words good? What's the best kind of talking? Why?

Older children and adults may read: Matthew 12:33–37

Let's pray: Dear God, please forgive all the words we say that may hurt someone. Help us understand how powerful words can be, and teach us to say only words that are helpful. Make us willing to talk a lot about our Lord Jesus. In His name we ask it. Amen.

Let the redeemed of the LORD say so. Psalm 107:2 (RSV)

What Would *You* Do?

It was the last day of school. All the books had been put away and the desks cleaned out, but there was still a little time left.

So Mr. Jackson passed out some paper. He told his students they were going to do one more lesson. "On your paper, write what you would do if this were the last day of your life," Mr. Jackson said. "Or what would you do tomorrow if you knew you would die the next day."

Austin wrote, "I'd be real nice to my sister so I could go to heaven."

"I'd have all the fun I could have," wrote James. "I'd eat a lot of ice cream and play and go swimming."

51

Allissa thought for awhile. Then she wrote, "If I had only one more day to live, I'd tell people about Jesus. You see, Jesus is my Savior, and I'd want other people to be saved too."

Which student wrote the best answer? Allissa, of course. Austin thought he could get to heaven by doing good things. James thought only about himself. Allissa thought of Jesus and wanted to help others get to heaven.

The Bible says, "Believe in the Lord Jesus, and you will be saved." It also says, "Whoever believes in Him shall not perish but have eternal life." To believe in Jesus means to trust that He is God and the Savior of all. That's why Allissa's answer was the best answer.

The psalm verse says, "Let the redeemed of the LORD say this—" What are they to say? They are to thank and praise God and say that they are redeemed, or saved. They should tell others that Jesus has saved the whole world by dying on the cross for all sins. Then more people will believe in Jesus and will be saved.

Let's talk: What did Mr. Jackson ask his students to write? What did Austin write? What did James write? What did Allissa write? Why did Allissa want to help save people? From what does Jesus save people? What does the psalm verse say?

Older children and adults may read: Psalm 107:1–9

Let's pray: Dear Father in heaven, we're glad that we're saved and belong to You. Help us tell others so that they will believe in Jesus and be saved too. In Jesus' name we pray this. Amen.

A righteous man cares for the needs of his animal, but the kindest acts of the wicked are cruel. Proverbs 12:10

Your Pets and You

"Mrs. Frank is giving collie pups away, Dad," said Makoto. "Can we get one?"

Dad looked Makoto in the eye and said, "Do you remember when we had a rabbit? Who had to feed him?"

"Mother did," answered Makoto. "But it'll be different this time."

"Once there was a boy who had a dog, but he never washed him, never fed him, and hardly ever played with him," Dad said. "The boy said he loved the dog, but he was really cruel to the animal."

"I won't be like that, Dad," Makoto promised.

"Okay," said Dad. "But I want you to learn a Bible verse. Please get me the Bible."

Makoto brought the Bible to his father, who turned to Proverbs 12:10. "As soon as you know that verse from memory and can tell me what it means, let me know," Dad said. "Then we'll talk about the dog."

Makoto learned the verse quickly and was even ready to explain it. "The first part says, 'A righteous man cares for the needs of his animal.' This means that we should give our animals enough to eat and clean water to drink and a nice place to stay, and we should treat them well," said Makoto.

"All right," said Dad. "How about the second part of the verse?"

"The second part means that it's wicked to forget your pet and not give him enough to eat and a good place to stay. That would be cruel even if you loved him and liked to play with him," explained Makoto.

"Very good," said Dad. "Now how about promising to take good care of your animal?"

"I promise," said Makoto, and so he got his puppy. And when he forgot to take care of his dog, Dad reminded him of the Bible verse he had learned.

⤚

Let's talk: What did Makoto want? What Bible verse did he learn? What did it mean? What kind of pets do you think Jesus might have had? How do you think Jesus treated His pets? Why do Christians want to treat their animals well?

Older children and adults may read: Proverbs 12:10–15

Let's pray: Please forgive us, dear heavenly Father, if we have been cruel to our animals by forgetting to take care of them or in other ways. Please give us more of Your Spirit and make us more kind to people and to our pets. In Jesus' name we pray. Amen.

Do not withhold discipline from a child. Proverbs 23:13

Why Kelly Wanted to Be Grounded

Kelly had been bad, and she knew it. Twice in one week her dad grounded her. She was young, but not so young that she didn't know why she was grounded.

Kelly told her friend Paolo about the groundings.

"I never get grounded," said Paolo.

"Sometimes you should get grounded," Kelly responded.

"Why?" asked Paolo.

" 'Cause then you'd be easier to play with, and you'd grow up to be a better person, and ... and ... you might get to be a Christian too," Kelly explained.

"Do groundings make you a Christian?" asked Paolo.

"No, but Dad says I'd get spoiled if he didn't ground me when I do things I know are wrong."

"I'm glad my dad doesn't ground me," Paolo said.

"I'm glad my dad grounds me when I need it," said Kelly. "I want to be good 'cause I belong to Jesus."

"Can't you belong to Him when you're bad?" asked Paolo.

"Sure," said Kelly. "But Jesus wants us to be sorry for the bad things we do. Groundings help you to be sorry because they give you time to think about what you did and how it hurt other people and Jesus."

The Bible tells parents not to withhold discipline from their children. Discipline keeps children from becoming spoiled and helps them learn to make good choices.

Good parents discipline only when their children need it because they love their children. And *because* they love God and their children, Christian parents try to correct their children when they do wrong.

Let's talk: Why was Kelly glad she got grounded? What did Paolo think about groundings? Who do you think was the better-behaved child? What does the Bible tell parents about disciplining their children? Why can we be glad when our parents correct us?

Older children and adults may read: Proverbs 23:22–25

Let's pray: Heavenly Father, help us learn from our punishments so that we will turn away from sin and stay close to You. We ask this because of Jesus, who died to save us. Amen.

[Don't be a] hearer that forgets but a doer that acts.
James 1:25 (RSV)

A Good Listener

Graces's mother was very surprised. "Why, Grace, you have the table all set!" she said.

"Isn't that what Pastor told me to do in his sermon Sunday?" asked Grace. She was trying to act as though she hadn't tried to surprise her mother.

"I don't remember that he said anything about setting the table," Mother answered.

"Well, he said that children please God by helping their parents," Grace explained. By now she couldn't help showing how happy her good deed had made her.

Maybe Grace didn't know it, but she was also being a good Bible listener. God's Word says we should all be good Bible listeners.

The apostle James said, "Don't be a hearer who forgets but a doer who acts." It doesn't help much to listen to a sermon if we don't do what the sermon says. Nor does it help to read the Bible or have family devotions if we don't try to live what we learn.

Grace was a hearer who acted when she set the table for her mother. How good a Bible listener are you? That depends on whether you do what the Bible says.

~

Let's talk: Why did Grace set the table for her mother? How did it make her feel? What kind of Bible listener could we say Grace was? What kind of hearer of God's Word are we to be? Memorize the Bible verse.

Older children and adults may read: James 1:22–27

Let's pray: Dear God, we often don't do what You have said in the Bible. Please forgive us for Jesus' sake. Help us do whatever we learn from You so that we will be happy hearers and learners of Your Word. For Jesus' sake we ask it. Amen.

What good thing must I do to get eternal life? Matthew 19:16

The Trouble Money Can Lead To

Colin was in New York City with his father. They were riding in a taxi. As they passed a big church, Colin's father leaned forward and asked the cab driver, "Did you ever go to this church?"

"Naw," said the driver. "I don't have time to go to church. I'm too busy trying to make money. If a preacher can tell me how to get more money, I'll go hear him."

Colin's father was surprised at what the man said. "Loving money leads to all kinds of evil," he told the driver. "That's a warning God gives us in the Bible."

"Yeah, I know," responded the driver. "But I love it. Money's all that matters. If you've got it, you can buy what you want, and people treat you well. But if you're poor, you're nothing."

Colin's father shook his head. He felt sorry for the cab driver. "I know you can't buy God," he said, "and you need Him." But the driver just gave a little huff.

Later Colin and his father talked about the man. "Colin, there are many things much more important than money. Can you name a few?" Father asked.

Colin didn't have to think very long. "You and my mother and being well and being happy and God and ..." Colin rattled off.

"Good for you," said Father. "I'm glad these things are

important to you. Nothing is more important than life with God. That's why we need to listen to what He says. You know what He says about life with Him, don't you?"

"Sure, Dad," said Colin. "People who believe that Jesus is their Savior have everlasting life. That's life with God."

"Good," said Father. "Don't ever let the love of money lead you away from Jesus. That's the worst thing that could happen."

Let's talk: What did the cab driver love more than God? Why? What showed that he probably wasn't a Christian? Why does God warn us about loving money? How can the love of money lead people to sin? What is the worst trouble money can lead us into?

Older children and adults may read: Matthew 19:16–22

Let's pray: Dear God and Father in heaven, we confess that we too have sometimes loved money more than we love You. Please forgive us for Jesus' sake because He died for this sin also. Lead us by the Holy Spirit to love You more than anything else and keep us from the sin of loving money. We ask this in Jesus' name. Amen.

Do not [just] listen to the word. ... Do what it says.
James 1:22

God's Mirror

"Travis Nelson, you go right to the bathroom and look in the mirror. You're a sight!" Travis' mother told her son. He had been playing in the park where it was muddy.

Travis looked in the mirror. There were dried mud spots all over his face. His clothes were muddy too and his hair was tangled.

Then Travis heard someone calling him from outside. His friend Donzell wanted to play. So Travis ran out the back door and forgot all about what he had seen in the mirror.

Looking in the mirror didn't do Travis much good, did it? Many people look into God's mirror that way. Even when they see the dirt in their life, they forget to do something about it.

Do you know what God's mirror is? It's God's Word. When a teacher teaches a Bible story, or the pastor preaches a sermon, or we have a family devotion, or we read our Bible, the Word of God is like a mirror.

When we hear Jesus say, "Love one another as I have loved you," we see that we haven't been as loving and kind as Jesus wants us to be. Or when we hear, "Be glad in the Lord always," we hear God saying how we should act, even though we know we've been grumpy. That's like looking in a mirror. The Word of God shows us what we do wrong.

But it doesn't do any good to look in a mirror and not do something about what we see. When our face is dirty, it needs to be washed. When our hair is tangled, it needs to be combed. When we see that God wants us to be kind, we need to ask Him to help us treat others with kindness.

When God tells us to be happy, we can ask Him to put joy in our hearts. The Bible says, "Do not [just] listen to the word. ... Do what it says."

Let's talk: What did Travis see when he looked in the mirror? Why didn't the mirror help him? What is God's mirror? How do we look in this mirror? Who is the only One who can wash away our sins? How does He do it?

Older children and adults may read: Matthew 7:21–27

Let's pray: Dear Father in heaven, please lead us to look in Your mirror often and to ask Jesus to wash away our sins. Help us also to walk in the ways that are right so that our lives will remain clean. We ask this for Jesus' sake. Amen.

Touch no unclean thing. 2 Corinthians 6:17

Books Can Kill

In India, a country far away, a soldier went to the library. The book he wanted was on a high shelf. When he reached for it, something bit him. The soldier jerked the book down, and a small snake fell out. Its bite was very dangerous.

The soldier quickly killed the snake, but his hand puffed up. He almost died from the poison.

There's another kind of poison in some books. When you read books with evil characters or a lot of violence, you are poisoning your mind and heart. These books can kill your life with God. They can make you think it's not so bad to hurt others or treat others badly.

The same thing can happen when you watch television shows that make evil look like fun. It isn't fun when it separates you from God.

If you knew there was a snake in a book, you wouldn't touch it, would you? If you knew you could be separated from God by a television program, would you watch it?

In the Bible, the apostle Paul gives us an even better reason for avoiding things that aren't good for us. He says that because we believe in Jesus, "we are the temple of the living God. As God has said, 'I will live in them and walk among them, and I will be their God, and they will be My people. Therefore ... touch no unclean thing. ... I will be a Father to you, and you will be My sons and daughters,' says the LORD Almighty."

We are children of God, and God is living in us. He

won't leave us because of one sin or because we read one bad book. But because God loves us so much, we want to love Him back. Let's not spoil that with anything bad that we might see or read.

$$\approx$$

Let's talk: What was in the soldier's book? What did the poison do to him? What kind of poison is in some books? What does the Bible verse say? What do you think this means? What reason does the apostle Paul give for avoiding things that aren't clean?

Older children and adults may read: 2 Corinthians 6:16–18

Let's pray: Dear Lord, our God, please help us avoid what isn't good for us to read and hear and see. Make us willing to turn away from what is evil because we are Your children through Jesus Christ, our Lord. Amen.

[Jesus said,] "This is my command: Love each other."
John 15:17

The Perfect Glue

Miss Martin came over and showed her neighbor, Mrs. Samuels, a box she had received in the mail. "They fooled me," Miss Martin said. "A newspaper ad offered to send a box of perfect glue free. And look what I got!"

Mrs. Samuels opened the box. Inside was a piece of paper. Written on the paper was one word: *Love.*

"The ad promised it would mend almost anything," said Miss Martin. She was a little angry.

"What they said is true in a way," Mrs. Samuels responded. "Love will mend almost anything, even broken hearts." Then they both laughed, and Miss Martin felt better.

People spend a lot of money for a nice house, for a television, rugs, and furniture. But if they don't put love into their house, it can never be a happy home. If they could buy love for as much as a car costs, what a bargain that would be!

Love is the best glue in the world, especially Christian love. It glues a family together. It helps them treat each other with kindness and mends the cracks that happen when things separate family members.

Jesus told His disciples, "This is My command: Love each other." God is love, so He wants us to love others. And love does wonders.

Before we say that mean word, remember that God wants us to say words of love. Before we make that sour face, remember that God would rather see a smile. Before we slam the door in anger, think of the love God wants us to show. He will help us speak and show love to others.

Love is the world's best glue—and it's *free!* We get all we need from God through Jesus—free of charge.

~

Let's talk: What did the paper say was the perfect glue? How is this true? What are some ways we use love in our home? What does Jesus command in our Bible verse? Who gives us all the love that we need?

Older children and adults may read: John 15:12–17

Let's pray: Dear God, we're glad that the very best thing for our home doesn't cost anything. Please make us willing to bring love into our home. Give us Your Holy Spirit so that we will love as Jesus wants us to love. We ask this in Jesus' name. Amen.

Jesus replied, "If anyone loves Me, he will obey My teaching." John 14:23

Real Love

"I love you, Mother," said Sasha. And she gave her mother a kiss and ran out to play. She didn't bother to pick up her toys as her mother had asked.

"I love you, Mom," said Andy and gave his mother a kiss. Then he went over to his friend's house and forgot all about straightening up his room and cutting the lawn.

"I love you, Mom," said Sergio. Then he helped his mom with the dishes and laughed and talked with her as they picked up the toys and books. When his little sister cried, Sergio played with her until his mom could feed her.

Which of the three children do you think loved their mother the most? Yes, it was the one who helped the most. It's so easy to *say*, "I love you," but what we *do* shows how much we *really* love.

And that's how it is with loving Jesus. Do you know what He said about loving Him? Jesus said, "If anyone loves Me, he will obey My teaching." Those who love Jesus gladly do what He has said they are to do. Real love is shown by doing, not by talking.

Let's talk: Which of the three children loved their mother the most? How could you tell? What did Jesus say we do if we love Him? How do we obey His words?

Older children and adults may read: John 14:21–24

Let's pray: Dear Lord Jesus, Your love for us wasn't only in words. You worked and suffered and died for us. Please forgive us for not always showing that we love You by what we do. Give us the Holy Spirit so that we can love You more and obey Your teaching.lAmen.

[The angel said,] "He is not here; He has risen, just as He said." Matthew 28:6

Napoleon and Jesus

A long time ago, a man named Napoleon became a famous ruler of France. His army won wars against many other people, so Napoleon and France ruled many other countries.

But God didn't let Napoleon stay powerful. After awhile, his army lost a war. The great ruler was captured and put on an island. He had to stay there until he died.

Years later, the French people brought Napoleon's body back to France. They wanted to remember their great leader. They put his body in six coffins, one inside the other, and placed it in a beautiful, big church.

Every day many people visit the church to look at Napoleon's coffin. But Napoleon is dead. He can't help the French people. Even when he was alive, he became great only by using force.

Jesus, our leader, is greater than Napoleon. He didn't force people to love Him. He died to save them. He also showed that He is more than just a man. He became alive again after He died and showed that He is really God.

When some women who were friends of Jesus came to the place where He had been buried, they found the grave empty. Instead of Jesus' body, there was an angel who said, "He is not here; He has risen, just as He said."

What a great leader we Christians have! Jesus is not someone who lived a long time ago—He's still living today! Jesus is not a proud ruler who *killed* people to become great—He is kind and loving. Jesus made Himself poor even though He's the king of heaven and earth. He died on a cross to save the whole world.

That's why the empty grave where Jesus was buried is a more wonderful place than the church where Napoleon is buried. That's why we talk about Napoleon, but we *worship* and *pray* to Jesus.

Let's talk: Who was Napoleon? What happened to him? Where is he buried now? Why do people visit the church where he is buried? Why can't he help the French people? Why is Jesus a greater leader than Napoleon ever was? How do Christians honor Jesus?

Older children and adults may read: Matthew 28:1–9

Let's pray: Lord Jesus, our living Savior and King, how glad we are that You rose from the dead and aren't buried in a grave. We thank You, dear Jesus, for saving us from our sins. Help us remember that You are still living and that we can trust You for help in any trouble. Someday take us to where You are in heaven, that we may live forever with You. Amen.

Knowledge puffs up, but love builds up. 1 Corinthians 8:1

The Best Report

"I'm the best student in our class," Jordan said as she showed her report card to her mother. "Do you know who the worst one is? Colleen. She almost never has her homework done, and sometimes she sleeps in class."

"I'm glad you have a good report card," Mother said. "But Colleen has a good report card too."

"She does? Did you see it?" asked Jordan.

"No, I didn't see it," answered Mother. "But I heard it from her mother."

"Mothers don't give report cards," said Jordan. She was glad because she knew she wasn't the best at helping her mother.

"Colleen's mother gave her a very good report card," said Jordan's mother. "She told me that Colleen helps her a lot. When she was sick, Colleen rocked her baby brother to sleep during the night. She also cleaned the house and tried to make the meals."

"Is that why she was so sleepy in school?" asked Jordan.

"Perhaps," replied Mother. "Anyway, Colleen is kind to her brother and helps her mother."

"I guess maybe Colleen has a better report card than I have," said Jordan.

There's a Bible verse that says, "Knowledge puffs up, but love builds up." Report cards may tell what we know, but they don't tell how we love. When we know things but don't love, we become proud and think we're important. But when we love, the Holy Spirit is working in us and building up our faith in Jesus.

How can we become more loving? By following Jesus' loving example. He is God, and God is love.

Let's talk: Who had the best report card? Who gave Colleen a good report card? Whose report card do you think God liked the best? What does the Bible say about knowledge? How does love build up a person? Who makes us more loving?

Older children and adults may read: 1 Corinthians 13. Use the word *love* in place of *charity* if that's the way your Bible reads. Years ago, *charity* meant *love*.

Let's pray: Dear Father in heaven, please help us learn our school lessons so that we'll be able to do our work well for You. More importantly, give us the Holy Spirit so that we will become more loving and helpful. Please do this for Jesus' sake. Amen.

Teach them to your children and to their children after them. Deuteronomy 4:9

Teaching Dolls to Pray

Tamara had five dolls. One day she had them all lined up along the side of her bed. They were on their knees, with their faces against the bed.

"What are they doing?" Aunt Eileen asked.

"They're praying," said Tamara, surprised that her aunt would have to ask.

"What are they praying for?" asked Aunt Eileen.

"They're praying for Joyce to get better so I can play with her again," Tamara answered.

"Let's all pray for that," said Aunt Eileen, and she put Tamara on her lap. "You and me and the dolls—let's all pray for Joyce."

"Dear God, please make Joyce well soon. And while she's sick, make her heart happy. Amen," prayed Aunt Eileen.

"I'm glad you pray for others," Tamara's aunt said. "I'm glad for something else too."

"What's that?" asked Tamara.

"I'm glad you were teaching your dolls to pray," Aunt Eileen said with a smile. "When you're big and God gives you children, I hope you will teach them to pray."

"I will," promised Tamara. "And I'll want them to know Bible stories, and all about Jesus, and the Ten Commandments, and everything."

Aunt Eileen was glad that Tamara was planning to be a Christian mother. God wants His children to teach their children the wonderful things that He has done. Do you know why? The psalm writer says so "they will put their trust in God and will not forget His deeds, but will keep His commands."

Let's talk: What were the dolls doing? Can dolls really pray? Why was Aunt Eileen glad to pray with Tamara and her dolls? What does God want His children to teach their children?

Older children and adults may read: Psalm 78:1–7

Let's pray: Dear God, please fill our minds with Your thinking and planning so that when we're older, we'll do what You have told us. Remind all parents to teach their children about the wonderful things You have done. Help us trust in Your love and obey Your commands. Help us for Jesus' sake. Amen.

My times are in [God's] hands. Psalm 31:15

Living in God's Hands

"Aren't you afraid to go there?" Becky asked Miss Roth. Miss Roth was Becky's teacher, and she was planning to work for God as a missionary in New Guinea. It was far away and Becky was scared she'd never see Miss Roth again.

"No, I'm not afraid," said Miss Roth. "Why should I be?"

"Somebody might kill you," said Becky, her eyes starting to fill with tears. "Or you may get sick and be far away from a hospital. Or a snake might bite you. I wouldn't like to live in that country. It's too dangerous."

"My times are in God's hands," said Miss Roth. "That's a Bible verse. It means that God knows what's best for His children. My life is in God's hands and I trust Him to do what's best for me."

"God doesn't expect me to go to New Guinea, does He?" asked Becky.

"I don't know what God expects of you, Becky," Miss Roth answered. "But I'm sure God wants me to go to New Guinea, so I'm glad to go for Him. Jesus did much more than that for me. He died for me. But no matter what I do or where I go, I don't have to worry because I'll be living in God's hands."

Becky started to think about what God might want her to do for Him. She wanted to live in God's hands too. Now she knew this meant following God's ways and doing His work, whatever that might be.

Let's talk: Did you ever see a little bird sit in someone's hand? Why does it feel safe? In whose hands did Miss Roth say her life was? Why wasn't she afraid to go to New Guinea? Why did she want to go? What did Becky begin to think about?

Older children and adults may read: Romans 10:9–15

Let's pray: Dear Father in heaven, please help us remember that our times are in Your hands. Give us the Holy Spirit so we'll gladly trust Your plan for our lives. Help us trust the love that You give us through Jesus. Make us glad to work for You and not be afraid. We ask this in Jesus' name. Amen.

They exchanged the truth of God for a lie. Romans 1:25

Changing Truth into Lies

"My mom is sick," Peter told Mrs. Munsey, the woman who lived across the street. "I asked God to make her well."

"Peter," said Mrs. Munsey, "your mother isn't sick. Nobody is ever really sick. They just think they're sick. And nobody ever dies."

"Jesus died," said Peter.

"No, He didn't," said Mrs. Munsey. "Nobody dies. They just become somebody else and keep on living. Here's a book for your mother to read. It will tell her that she isn't sick."

"I'll take it to Mom, but I know she's sick," Peter said. "And I know that Jesus died. He died to pay for my sins. And He became alive again."

Peter went home and told his mom what Mrs. Munsey had said. "Peter, those people mean well, but they don't believe the Bible," Mom explained. "They'd rather believe books that have changed God's truth into a lie."

"I knew she was wrong all the time," said Peter.

"I'm glad you did," said Mom. "We'd be very foolish to trade God's truth for a lie."

"That isn't a good trade, is it?" said Peter.

"No," Mom answered. "It's not even as good as when you traded your telescope for some marbles."

⤴

Let's talk: What did Mrs. Munsey believe? What did Peter believe? Who was right? How do we know who is right? What did Peter's mom tell him?

Older children and adults may read: Romans 1:18–25

Let's pray: Lord God, please keep us from ever changing Your truth into a lie. Help all who believe lies to learn the truth, especially the truth about Jesus and life with You. We ask this in Jesus' name. Amen.

Love never fails. 1 Corinthians 13:8

For God, Not for Thanks

"I don't think I'll do any more favors for Malcolm. He never even says thank you," Devon told his father.

"What kind of favors do you do for Malcolm?" asked Dad.

"Oh, like holding his books when he takes off his coat," said Devon. "Or giving him the homework assignments when he's sick."

"Why did you do these favors for him in the first place?" asked Dad.

" 'Cause I wanted to be nice to him, and I should be kind," answered Devon.

"Well, if you should do nice things, don't you think you should do them even if Malcolm never says thank you?" asked Dad.

"But he never does anything for me," complained Devon.

"But if it's what you should do, does it depend on a thank you?" Dad asked again.

"I guess not, but it sure would be easier," said Devon.

"I'm sure it would," agreed Dad. "But why don't you do good for God and not for thanks? You could say to yourself, 'I'm holding Malcolm's books for Jesus. I'm helping Malcolm because I'm a Christian.' Then you won't get tired of doing favors."

It's easy to show love when somebody is nice. But Christian love goes on doing good even when love doesn't come back. The Bible says, "Love never fails." That's a short Bible verse worth remembering. Say those three words a few times. They'll help you understand God's kind of love.

Let's talk: Why did Devon get tired of doing favors for Malcolm? What did Devon's dad tell him? What does our Bible verse tell us about real love? Who gives us the kind of love that never fails?

Older children and adults may read: Romans 12:9–21

Let's pray: Heavenly Father, help us remember how good You are even to people who never thank You. Jesus even died for them too. Make us willing to do good for Jesus' sake, whether we are thanked for it or not. In His name we pray. Amen.

Anyone, then, who knows the good he ought to do and doesn't do it, sins. James 4:17

The Sin of Doing Nothing

Stuart lived near a road that crossed a stream. One year it rained so much that the bridge washed away.

"You'd better put some boards over the stream so people won't have to walk through the water," Stuart's wife told him.

But Stuart was too lazy. "Why should I drag heavy boards down there for a bunch of other people?" he asked.

So Stuart did nothing.

When people came down the road, they had to walk through the water. One man ruined a good pair of shoes. A lady ruined her pants. A boy got very sick because his feet got wet when it was cold.

Whose fault was it that these things happened? Stuart's. He could have laid those boards across the stream until the bridge was fixed.

Did Stuart think he had done anything wrong? "Me?" Stuart probably would have said. "I didn't do nothing." But Stuart's sin was doing nothing when he could have done something.

When you can do something good and you don't do it,

that's sin. The Bible says, "Anyone, then, who knows the good he ought to do and doesn't do it, sins." When people say, "I didn't do nothing," that may mean they didn't do what they could have.

Jesus died to pay for this kind of sin too. And for Jesus' sake God forgives the sin of not doing what we could to help others. But because Jesus came to help us, we can follow His example and help others.

Let's talk: What should Stuart have done about the bridge? Why didn't he do it? How did his laziness hurt other people? Why was this Stuart's fault? Can you think of other examples when it's wrong to do nothing? Why does God forgive the sin of not doing what we can?

Older children and adults may read: Luke 10:30–37

Let's pray: Dear Father in heaven, please help us love people so that we won't try to find excuses but will gladly help in any way we can. Help us follow Jesus' example. In His name we pray. Amen.

"Call upon Me in the day of trouble." Psalm 50:15

Mrs. Bridges in Trouble

Mrs. Bridges was having a lot of trouble. Her husband had died. She was behind in her house payments. Her car had been taken away. And her daughter was sick.

"I just don't know what to do," Mrs. Bridges told Mr. Noland.

"We'll help you in any way we can, but why don't you also pray to God about it?" said Mr. Noland.

"I wish I could," responded Mrs. Bridges. "I don't think I should. You see, I haven't prayed to God for a long time."

"Then isn't it time for you to pray now?" asked Mr. Noland.

"But I forgot about God when things were going well. It isn't fair to think of God only when things don't go right," Mrs. Bridges said.

"That's true," Mr. Noland said. "But God wants you to pray to Him anyway."

"Are you sure God wants me to pray to Him?" asked Mrs. Bridges. She really wanted to believe what Mr. Noland had said.

"God says so," Mr. Noland told her. "In the Bible, He says, 'Call upon Me in the day of trouble.' It's Psalm 50:15. And that isn't all He said. He also said, 'I will deliver you.' That's a promise to help and save you. And God keeps His promises."

"I'm sorry I didn't stay in touch with God," said Mrs. Bridges.

Mr. Noland smiled. "God sometimes lets troubles come to us so we won't forget Him," he said. "You see, He wants to save us from our worst trouble—our sins and their punishment. That's why Jesus died for us."

"Did Jesus really die for me too?" asked Mrs. Bridges.

"Yes, He did. The Bible says, 'He died for all.' And when you belong to Jesus, God forgives your sins and loves you for Jesus' sake," Mr. Noland told her.

That night Mrs. Bridges called to God for help in her troubles.

Let's talk: What kind of troubles did Mrs. Bridges have? What did Mr. Noland tell her to do? Why didn't she want to pray? How does God invite us to pray when we're in trouble? What does God promise to do for those who call to Him for help? How do you think He helped Mrs. Bridges?

Older children and adults may read: Psalm 130

Let's pray: Dear God, thank You for letting us pray to You in our Savior Jesus' name. We're glad that You always answer us in some way, even though we don't deserve it. We thank You especially for promising to save us from our sins because we trust in Jesus. In His name we pray. Amen.

Who has known the mind of the Lord? Romans 11:34

How Mario Fixed a Clock

The kitchen clock was running a little slow.

"I'm going to save Dad some money. I'll fix it myself," said Mario. So he took the clock apart and looked it over. But he couldn't see anything wrong or broken.

Then Mario tried to put the clock together again. When he was finished, he had three wheels left over. Mario didn't know where they belonged. He also had two screws left. Now the clock wouldn't run at all.

"I guess I don't understand clocks," said Mario. "Can

you get it fixed, Dad?" he asked. They took it to someone who knew how to fix clocks.

"It isn't easy to understand a clock, is it?" Mario's dad said on the way home.

Mario felt a little ashamed of what he had done. "I thought I knew how to fix it," he answered.

"You're a little like the people who think they understand God. They think they know all about everything," said Dad. "They also think they know how God should do things. They try to tell Him what to do."

"And they couldn't even figure out a clock if they had to," said Mario, laughing at himself.

"I think this teaches us to trust God. He knows what He's doing, even when we can't understand Him," Dad told Mario. "The Bible says, 'Who has known the mind of the Lord?' "

"Jesus knows," said Mario, "because He's the Lord."

"You're right!" said Dad. "That's why we'd better let Jesus tell us about God and life with Him."

Let's talk: What did Mario try to fix? Why did he have some parts left over? What question does the Bible verse ask? What's the answer? Where does God tell us what He wants us to know? How do we let the Lord Jesus decide things for us?

Older children and adults may read: Romans 11:33–36

Let's pray: Dear heavenly Father, if we can't understand such simple things as clocks, how can we hope to understand You? Please help us trust You, no matter what happens. Help us turn our lives over to You. We're glad that You love us for Jesus' sake, and that's really all we need to know. In Jesus' name. Amen.

If we have food and clothing, we will be content.
1 Timothy 6:8

When Nobody Was Satisfied

A rich man put an advertisement in a newspaper. It said: "I will give a house to the first person who is satisfied with what he has."

Many people came and asked for the house. When the man asked why they wanted it, the people told him that the house they had was too small, or that it wasn't their own, or that it wasn't paid for. They all wanted something better than they had.

"You're not satisfied with what you have," the man told these people. So he gave the house to a widow with five children who was working hard but didn't make much money. She didn't ask for the house.

Are most people satisfied? No, they aren't. When they have a car, they want a better one. When they have a job, they wish they didn't have to work. When they don't have something to do, they wish they could work.

Children, too, are often not satisfied. When they're on

vacation, they want to be home. When they're home, they want to go somewhere. Sometimes children are unhappy when they can't have what they see in a store or on television.

It isn't always wrong to want things. Jesus even told us to ask Him for much more than we do. But God doesn't want us to be unhappy if we can't have what we want.

As long as we have enough to eat and enough to wear and a place to live, we can be satisfied. If God gives us more, we can be thankful. If that's all He wants us to have, we can trust that God knows what's best. That's why the apostle Paul says in our Bible verse: "If we have food and clothing, we will be content."

Let's talk: What did the rich man advertise? Why didn't the people who came get the house? Who got it? Why are most people never satisfied? Why can we be satisfied with whatever God gives us? What did the apostle Paul tell Timothy in the Bible verse?

Older children and adults may read: 1 Timothy 6:6–11

Let's pray: Dear Lord God, we thank You for the many things You have given us. Please forgive our grumbling and complaining. Help us to be thankful for what You give us. Make us satisfied with what You think is best. We ask this in Jesus' name. Amen.

[We are] poor, yet making many rich. 2 Corinthians 6:10

How to Make Others Rich

"I'm going to marry Curt Harris; he'll make me rich," said Maria. And she did marry him. Because Curt Harris was rich, he made Maria rich.

But the two weren't happy together. They didn't love each other. Making someone rich with money doesn't always make that person happy.

In the Bible, the apostle Paul tells of another way to make people rich. Even someone who is poor can make a person rich the Bible way. Though Paul was poor, he wrote, "We make many rich."

What did Paul mean? How did he make people rich? He and his helpers were poor people. They didn't have a lot of money. They didn't own a lot of things or a big business.

Paul told people about Jesus. Through Paul's words, the Holy Spirit led people to faith in Jesus as their Savior. From Jesus they received the forgiveness of their sins and a place in heaven. That's worth more than all the money in the world.

Jesus also gives us peace with God and joy in our hearts. He fills our hearts with love and helps us obey His teaching. This makes our hearts and lives rich.

We can help make people rich, just as Paul did. We can tell others about Jesus and His love. We too can help make people rich even though we may be poor.

Let's talk: Why did Maria marry Curt? How did he make her rich? Why didn't that make her happy? Who said he was poor but made people rich? How did the apostle Paul make people rich? How can we make people rich?

Older children and adults may read: 2 Corinthians 6:1–10

Let's pray: Dear Jesus, thank You for giving us forgiveness of sins and a happy life with God. Help us make other people rich in the same way by telling them of Your love. Amen.

God loves a cheerful giver. 2 Corinthians 9:7

The Happy Giver

"If you had a million dollars, would you give part of it to Jesus?" Mrs. Watson asked her Sunday school class.

They all said they would.

"If you had $500, would you give $300 to Jesus?" Mrs. Watson asked.

"Yes," her students answered, "we would."

"If you had one dollar, would you give part of it to Jesus?" Mrs. Watson asked again.

Her students looked at each other. "Yes," said Timothy. But what he didn't say was that he didn't have a dollar to give.

"I would too," said Jeffrey, and he took a quarter out of his pocket and put it in the offering basket.

The other students kept quiet. They had money at home, but they didn't want to give part of it away, not even to their church. The children all said they would give part

of their million dollars because they didn't have it. But most of them didn't want to give what they could.

It's easy to say what we would do for Jesus if we had a million dollars. But how much will we do for Jesus with what we actually have? That's the real question and the real test. We show our love for God by what we're willing to do for Him right here and now.

Jesus wants us to give money or anything else to Him because we love Him, not because we have to. The Bible says, "God loves a cheerful giver." Cheerful givers are people who give because they want to. Because they know Jesus even gave His life for them, cheerful givers happily do what they can for Jesus and for others.

Let's talk: Why was the Sunday school class willing to give a part of their million dollars? Why didn't most of the children want to give part of one dollar? What do you think Jesus cares about most—our money or our love? Why are people who love Jesus cheerful givers? Memorize the Bible verse.

Older children and adults may read: Luke 7:36–50

Let's pray: Dear Jesus, help us remember that You love a cheerful giver. Make us glad to do what we can for You and for other people because we love You. Amen.

The word of the LORD came to Elijah: "Go and present your-self to Ahab." ... So Elijah went. 1 Kings 18:1–2

A Very Brave Person

Keitaro was only 3 years old the first time his parents wanted him to go to Sunday school by himself. He didn't

 85

want to go. He was afraid. He cried. But Mother said, "Jesus wants you to go, and He'll be with you." So Keitaro went.

Keitaro was brave that morning he went to Sunday school alone for the first time. People have to be brave to go where they're afraid to go. When Keitaro grows up, maybe he'll be as brave as the prophet Elijah was long ago.

Elijah told King Ahab and his wicked queen that there wouldn't be any rain for a long time. God was punishing them and their country for not obeying Him. And for three years it didn't rain. King Ahab and the queen blamed Elijah. They wanted to kill him, and they looked everywhere for him. But nobody knew where Elijah was. He was safe. God had told him where to hide.

One day the Lord told Elijah to present himself to Ahab. But that would be very dangerous. Elijah might be killed. Ahab had already killed most of the other prophets of the Lord. But the Bible says, "Elijah went." He didn't give any excuses. Because God told him to go, he went.

Those two words, "Elijah went," tell us what a brave man Elijah was. Elijah trusted God a lot when he went to see the king who wanted to kill him.

There are times when we also will have to be brave. To be brave doesn't mean doing things without being afraid. Brave people are sometimes very afraid. But when we're afraid and we do what God wants anyway, that's being brave.

Sometimes we have to be brave and say no to something we know is wrong even when others want us to say yes. Sometimes we have to be brave to do what God wants us to do. But God will give us the strength to be brave. He promises to hear us when we call for help. He also promises to save us from our troubles.

Some boys wanted Tyler to steal a bike. When Tyler

refused, they called him a chicken. But Tyler was brave. He didn't steal just because someone called him a name. God helps His children to be brave. And He takes care of them too, just as He took care of Elijah.

Let's talk: What was the brave prophet's name? Why was he hiding? What did God tell him to do? What does the Bible say Elijah did? Can you think of something brave we could do for God?

Older children and adults may read: 1 Kings 17:1–6; 18:1–8, 17–18

Let's pray: Dear Father in heaven, so often we are cowards when we should be brave. Please forgive us for Jesus' sake. Make us brave enough to do whatever You want us to do. We ask this in Jesus' name, who was brave enough to die for us. Amen.

One died for all, and therefore all died. 2 Corinthians 5:14

All Paid Up

All the children were in trouble. They had gone fishing where they weren't supposed to fish. They had thought it was alright, but it wasn't. It was against the law, and they were caught. Now each one had to pay a $30 fine.

Carri and Nathan and some of the others didn't have $30. "I don't even have $10," said Nathan. The group had gathered at Carri's house to discuss their problem.

Carri's father felt sorry for them, so he said, "I'll pay your fines for you."

"All of ours?" asked Nathan. "Mine too?"

"Yes, yours too," he answered.

"Wow! Thanks a lot," said Nathan. "Thanks a whole lot."

All the other children also thanked Carri's dad. "You have such a great dad!" they told Carri.

When the newspaper came the next day, Nathan sat at the kitchen table reading it. "Here's my name and all our names," he told his mom. "It says we all paid our fines. But we really didn't. It was Carri's dad who paid them all."

"Well, Nathan," said Mom, "if he paid the fine for you, that's the same as if you paid it. And if he paid for all, then everyone has paid."

"Isn't that great!" said Nathan.

"It's like what Jesus did for all of us," said Nathan's mom. "He paid the fines we owe God for breaking His laws. He didn't just pay money—He gave His life."

Jesus died to pay our fines. The Bible says, "He died for all." Because Jesus died for all, our fines are all paid. It's just as if we ourselves died to pay for our sins.

⤚

Let's talk: What had Carri, Nathan, and their friends done wrong? What was their punishment? Who paid it? What did the kids think of Carri's dad? What did the newspaper say? Who died to pay for what we have done wrong? What does our Bible verse say? How does this make us feel about Jesus?

Older children and adults may read: 2 Corinthians 5:14–21

Let's pray: Dear Jesus, how can we ever thank You enough for dying for us? Because You died for all of us, it's as if we paid for our sins. Help us understand this and show our thanks to You. Amen.

Even Christ did not please Himself. Romans 15:3

Me First?

Lakeisha was the leader, and she wanted things her way. "Now we'll play hide-and-seek," she said, and everyone played.

"Now we'll play ranch, and I'll be the rancher," Lakeisha said. So everyone played ranch.

Soon Lakeisha's friends got tired of playing what she wanted. "Let's play something else," they said.

But Lakeisha wouldn't listen. "You have to do what I want," she said. "I'm the leader." So one after another, her friends went to Carlton's house and played there.

Now Lakeisha was all alone. She went inside and told

her mother what happened. "No wonder they left you," Mother said. "Nobody likes people who always want their own way."

"Would Jesus let other people have their way?" asked Lakeisha.

"He certainly would in a game," said Mother. "The Bible says, 'Even Christ did not please Himself.' Whatever He did, He did to please His Father in heaven or us. He even suffered and died for us."

Then Lakeisha decided she would try to please her friends, not just herself. She would do it first of all to please Jesus. And when Lakeisha tried to please her friends, she found that it made others happy to be with her. This made her happier too.

Let's talk: How did Lakeisha try to please herself? Why did her friends go to Carlton's house? What did Lakeisha's mother tell her? What did Lakeisha decide to do? What happened when she stopped trying to please herself?

Older children and adults may read: Philippians 2:1–11

Let's pray: Lord Jesus, we're glad You didn't live to please Yourself. Instead, You even died for us. Please give us a love like Yours so that we will want to please You in everything we do. Make us want to please other people too and not just ourselves. We ask this for Your sake. Amen.

Store up for yourselves treasures in heaven. Matthew 6:20

Treasures in Heaven

Once there were two brothers who grew up together in England. One of them became a businessman and made lots of money. When he died, very few people cared, and hardly anyone ever thinks about him anymore.

The other brother became a doctor and a missionary. He went to Africa. He never had much money. He died a poor man. But he was rich in another way. People still talk about him often.

The brother who went to Africa was David Livingstone. He helped many people. He taught them about Jesus. He explored the country of Africa. He helped set many slaves free. Because of what he did for God and people, he is buried in a church in England along with kings and queens and other great people.

If it hadn't been for David Livingstone, we probably never would have heard about his brother. When his brother died, people said, "He was David Livingstone's brother."

David Livingstone's brother may have had some of God's treasures too, but which brother do you think had the best life? What kind of treasures would you rather have at the end of your life?

Jesus said, "Do not store up for yourselves treasures on earth." Don't spend your time just trying to get money or other things that thieves can steal. "But store up for yourselves treasures in heaven." Treasure God's love and God's Spirit. Thieves can't steal God's love or take your faith in Jesus away.

≈

Let's talk: How did one of the Livingstone brothers get rich? Why did the other brother remain poor? Where was David Livingstone's treasure? Which of the two brothers did the most for other people? What did Jesus say about treasures? What did He mean?

Older children and adults may read: Matthew 6:19–34

Let's pray: Dear Father in heaven, please lead us to store up treasures in heaven. More than anything, we want Your love and Spirit. It is worth more than all the money in the world. Through Your love, please make us rich in good works, for Jesus' sake. Amen.

A quick-tempered man does foolish things. Proverbs 14:17

Keep Your Temper: No One Wants It

"You get out of here," Cole yelled at his sister and pushed her. Amanda fell against the coffee table and hit her head. It started to bleed.

Cole got scared and ran outside. Amanda ran screaming to her mother, who washed the cut and put a Band-Aid on it.

Cole's mother didn't say anything to him when he crept quietly back into the house. Later that afternoon, when Amanda was taking her nap, Cole told his mom he was worried about Amanda and sorry he lost his temper.

Mom put her arm around Cole and said, "Don't you wish you didn't have that quick temper?"

"Yes," Cole whispered.

"You know, you might hurt somebody pretty bad someday because you get angry so easily," Mom said.

"I said I was sorry," Cole said hoarsely. Mom could tell he meant it because he had been crying.

"Then let's ask God to help us keep from getting angry," said Mom. So they asked God to forgive Cole for Jesus' sake, and they asked God to help Cole control his temper.

The Bible says, "A quick-tempered man does foolish things." When we get angry easily and lose our temper, we do wrong things that we wouldn't usually do.

When Jesus lived on earth, He kept His temper perfectly. We can ask Him to help us avoid getting angry.

Let's talk: Why did Cole push Amanda? What happened to her? Why was Cole sorry? How did Mom try to help Cole? Why will God forgive Cole? What does the Bible verse say about a person with a quick temper?

Older children and adults may read: Genesis 4:1–8

Let's pray: Dear Father in heaven, we know that You don't want people to have bad tempers. Please help us control ours so that we won't do anything foolish because we get angry easily. Forgive our sins for Jesus' sake. Send Your Holy Spirit to guide our actions and words so that we'll be easier to live with. In Jesus' name. Amen.

The Lord's will be done. Acts 21:14

When Natasha Grumbled

Natasha was standing by a window in her house, grumbling. "I don't understand it," she said. "I prayed for a nice day for our picnic, and look at it rain!"

"Maybe somebody else prayed for rain," said Philippe, teasing her.

Natasha pushed her lip out farther. Then she turned to her mother and asked, "Mom, why didn't Jesus let us have a good day? I prayed for it."

"He did give us a good day," answered Mom. "A rainy day is a good day. Today the strawberries are growing so you can have strawberry jam. Today the grass is growing so you can have milk and meat from cows that eat grass. Today the streets are being washed clean of dust and dirt. It's really a great day."

"But I want to have a picnic," Natasha said and stomped her feet.

"It isn't always good to get what we want," Mom said. "You prayed for a good day for your picnic, but maybe Mr. Neeman prayed for rain for his garden. What do you think God should do if gardens need rain and you want a picnic?"

"Well, all right," said Natasha without answering the question. "Let's have a picnic *tomorrow.*"

"Good girl," said Mom.

The Bible tells about a time when some Christians realized they couldn't have their way. Instead of complaining, they said, "Let the Lord's will be done." So we know that God loves us, and He wants to give us the best things. We can say to God, "Your will be done," and trust that He will do it. When we say this and mean it, we can be happy, no matter what happens. Let the Lord's will be done.

⁓

Let's talk: Why was Natasha grumbling? Why did her mother say it was a great day? Why isn't it always good to get what we want? Whose will is always good? What did some Christians in the Bible say should be done? Why can we happily say to God, "Your will be done"? How will this help us?

Older children and adults may read: 2 Corinthians 12:7–10

Let's pray: Please forgive us, dear God, for sometimes grumbling about what You decide. We're glad that You know what's best for us. Please help us accept Your decisions and willingly pray, "Your will be done." We ask this in Jesus' name. Amen.

Whoever keeps the whole law and yet stumbles at just one point is guilty of breaking all of it. James 2:10

The Lawbreaker

Mr. Gordon was trying to show his daughter Lauren that all people are sinners and that she sinned too. "Once in a while I do something wrong," Lauren admitted. "But I do a lot of good things too."

"Okay, suppose my secretary passed my desk 50 times. Each time she wanted to take $10 out of it, but she didn't. Would you call that being good 50 times?" Dad asked.

"Yes," said Lauren.

"But suppose the next time she walked by, she opened the desk and took $10," said Dad. "Would she be stealing?"

"She'd be a thief," said Lauren.

"But she didn't steal 50 times, she only stole once. Why don't you say she's 50 times better than a thief?" Dad asked.

"She's a thief even if she stole only once," Lauren answered.

"Right," said Dad. "And that's the way God figures it too. He says, 'Whoever keeps the whole law and yet stumbles at just one point is guilty of breaking all of it.' "

"Then I'm guilty of breaking God's law too," said Lauren, finally understanding.

"Yes, that's what the Bible means when it says, 'All have sinned,' " Dad said. "We're all sinners, and we all need God's forgiveness. And God forgives us for Jesus' sake."

"I admit it. I'm a sinner," said Lauren. "And I'm really glad that God forgives me because of Jesus."

Let's talk: Why did Lauren think she was good? What made the secretary a thief? What does the Bible verse say about anyone who breaks a single part of God's law? Why do we all need God's forgiveness? Why does God forgive us? How did this make Lauren feel?

Older children and adults may read: James 2:8–13

Let's pray: Dear God, please send Your Holy Spirit to show us that we are sinners and that we have a Savior—Jesus. May we show our thanks for His death that won our forgiveness in all that we do. In His name we pray. Amen.

[God] remembers that we are dust. Psalm 103:14

Remembering that We Are Dust

"Dad, why does the Bible say, 'God remembers that we are dusty'?" Eric asked as he got in the car at school.

"I don't recall the Bible saying that," said Dad. "Are you sure you didn't get something wrong?"

"It does too say that," said Eric. When they got home, Eric pulled his Bible out of his backpack. Quickly he looked for Psalm 103, the psalm his teacher had read that day.

Dad looked at the psalm. "Read verse 14 again, Eric," he said. "Does it say we are dusty?"

Eric, who was just learning to read, read the verse slowly, "He remembers that we are dusty, I mean, dust."

"That sounds better," said Dad. "When God created Adam, how did He do it?"

"He took some ground and shaped it like a man. Then God breathed into him God made him alive," Eric explained.

"Good, you remember the story," said Dad. "So Adam

was created out of ground. Dry ground is called dust. Adam's body wasn't made out of some heavenly stuff—and neither are we. So when we do something wrong, God remembers that we are only dust. That means God knows how easy it is for us to sin."

The same psalm says that "as a father has compassion on his children, so the LORD has compassion on those who fear Him." God felt sorry for us and sent His Son, Jesus, to save us. For Jesus' sake, God forgives our sins and makes us His children. How glad we are that God remembers we are made out of dust.

Let's talk: What mistake did Eric make when he read the Bible verse? How did God create Adam? What does God mean when He says He remembers that we are dust? What has He done for us because He has compassion on us? Why is God willing to forgive us?

Older children and adults may read: Psalm 103:8–14

Let's pray: Lord, our God, You know how easy it is for us to sin. Have mercy on us, Lord. For the sake of Jesus, please forgive all our sins as You have promised. Help us act like Your children in all that we do, even though we are weak and sinful. In Jesus' name we ask it. Amen.

More are the children of the desolate woman than of her who has a husband. Isaiah 54:1

A Family of 48 Children

Rose was only 22 years old when she finished college and decided to become a Christian teacher in a faraway country.

"Don't do it," her friends told Rose. "You won't have a chance to get married or have children if you go so far away."

"But I think God wants me to go," Rose said, and she went.

Rose didn't get married. But because she loved God and children, God gave her more children than most married women ever have. This is how it happened.

A woman who didn't believe in God had twins. The people in the village thought a bad spirit had made the twins. They put the twins under some bushes and left them both to die. Rose found the twins and took them home.

Another time a mother chased her son out of his home and told him never to come back. Rose gave him a place in her home and took care of him.

That's the way Rose's family started to grow. Soon Rose needed a big house for all her "children." Before she died, she had 48 sons and daughters. Rose taught all of them about Jesus and His love. Many of them are now missionaries.

Long ago, God's prophet said, "More are the children of the desolate woman than of her who has a husband." God often gives big families to people who aren't married but who love and help others.

And there's another way that God gives children to His people. When the Holy Spirit works faith in Jesus in people's hearts, they are born again. They become Christians. If we have helped them become God's children by telling them about Jesus, or by taking them to church or Sunday school, then in a way, they are also our children.

Let's talk: Where did Rose go? How did she get her first "children"? How did her family grow? How can a woman who isn't married have more children than a married woman? How can we help people become God's children?

Older children and adults may read: Isaiah 54:1–5

Let's pray: Dear Father above, we're glad that You have made us part of Your big family. Give us the Holy Spirit so that we will gladly help other people, especially children, learn about Your love and about Jesus. We ask this in Jesus' name. Amen.

Seek the LORD while He may be found; call on Him while He is near. Isaiah 55:6

Don't Wait

"Mr. Gilbert is next door visiting his grandkids," Darren announced. "I hope he'll let me come to his farm this summer. I love to ride the horses and hunt eggs and watch the pigs."

"Well, then you'd better go talk to him," said Mother.

"I will," said Darren, "as soon as I finish this story."

When he finished the story, Darren started putting a model airplane together. "Better go see Mr. Gilbert now," said Mother.

"I will, as soon as I finish my model," said Darren. When Darren finally went to see Mr. Gilbert, he was gone. Darren didn't get to go to his farm.

Some people think they have plenty of time to get to know God. Even though they want to live with Him in heaven, they always have something else to do that seems more important than calling on God here on earth. Some of them die without ever meeting God or getting acquainted with Him. They miss going to heaven.

That's why the prophet Isaiah said, "Seek the LORD while He may be found; call on Him while He is near." God sent His Holy Spirit to work faith in our hearts. He adopts us as His children and promises to take us to be with Him in heaven.

Let's talk: Why did Darren lose his chance to have fun on Mr. Gilbert's farm? Why do some people put off getting to know God? What will happen to people who don't seek the Lord? Who helps us turn to the Lord? Why will God have mercy on us?

Older children and adults may read: Isaiah 55:1–7

Let's pray: Heavenly Father, forgive us for visiting with You so little, even though You are always with us. Thank You for loving us so much that You sent Jesus to be our

Savior. Please turn us away from all sins so we can live happily with You both now and forever in heaven. In Jesus' name we ask it. Amen.

When I am afraid, I will trust in You. Psalm 56:3

In the Operating Room

Martina was very sick. She was in the hospital for an operation. The doctor had to take out her appendix so she could get better. A nurse was ready to give Martina a shot that would make her go to sleep during the operation.

"Are you going to put me to sleep?" Martina asked.

"Yes," said the nurse.

"Well, I always pray before I go to sleep," said Martina. "May I pray first?"

"Sure," said the nurse.

"Dear Jesus, please be with me while I'm asleep," Martina prayed. "Help the doctor do her work right. I know that You love me, dear Jesus, so please take care of me. Amen."

Martina smiled, and the nurse gave her the shot.

Jesus blessed the operation, and soon Martina was better. When she was ready to leave the hospital, the doctor told Martina's father, "I wish more adults would be as close to God as your daughter. I don't think you were afraid, were you, Martina?"

"No, I wasn't afraid. I asked Jesus to be with me, and I knew He would be," Martina answered. "Nothing could go wrong. If I had died, I would have gone to heaven."

The psalm writer said, "When I am afraid, I will trust in

God." In another psalm, King David said to God, "Those who know Your name will trust in You."

Because Martina knew that God loved her, she trusted that God wouldn't let anything bad happen. That's why she wasn't afraid, even of the operation.

Let's talk: Why was Martina in the hospital? What did she ask the nurse before she gave her the shot? What did she ask Jesus? Why wasn't Martina afraid? Memorize the Bible verse.

Older children and adults may read: Philippians 1:19–21

Let's pray: Dear God, we're glad that You love us and that You are always with us. We know that nothing bad can ever happen to us. Give us Your Holy Spirit so that when we are afraid, we'll trust in You. Bless us and keep us, through Jesus Christ, our Savior. Amen.

Do not judge, and you will not be judged. Luke 6:37

Little Lies and Big Harm

"Mom, Sara took my doll," said Whitney, with tears in her eyes. "She stealed it."

"Are you sure?" Mom asked.

"Uh-huh," Whitney sniffed. "We were sitting on the porch. I went inside to get some more doll clothes, and now Sara is gone and so's my doll."

"Let's go look," said Mom. Together they went to the porch and looked for the doll.

"There's my doll," Whitney said. She pointed under the chair and smiled. "Sara must have put her there to go to sleep."

But Mom wasn't smiling.

"Whitney, do you know you weren't very nice just now?" she asked.

"How was I bad, Mom?" Whitney asked.

"You told a lie about Sara, didn't you?" Mom said.

"You mean 'cause Sara *didn't* take my doll?" Whitney asked.

"Yes, and if we wouldn't have looked, you would still be thinking a lie about Sara," Mom explained. "Maybe you would be telling other people that Sara took your doll. Then they would think Sara steals."

"Would that be my fault, Mom?" asked Whitney.

"Yes, it would be, honey," Mom answered. "Jesus calls it 'judging.' Jesus said, 'Do not judge, and you will not be judged.' That means we shouldn't say things that aren't true or that could hurt other people. We should always treat others as we want to be treated. You wouldn't want Sara to call you a thief, would you?"

"Oh, no!" Whitney said. "I'm sorry I said Sara took my doll."

"I'm glad you're sorry," said Mom. "I forgive you and so does Jesus. But let's ask Him to help you keep from judging other people."

So Whitney and her Mom prayed.

❧

Let's talk: What did Whitney say about Sara? Where was the doll? What did Mom say to Whitney? How could Whitney's words have hurt Sara? What did Jesus say in our Bible verse? What does this mean? Why did Jesus forgive Whitney?

Older children and adults may read: Luke 6:36–38

Let's pray: Dear Father in heaven, we often think and say bad things about others. Please forgive us for Jesus' sake. Help us remember how such words can hurt people. Give us the Holy Spirit to help us avoid hurting others with the things we say. We ask this in Jesus' name. Amen.

[God] called you ... through our gospel.
2 Thessalonians 2:14

How God Calls

"Benito! O Benito!" his mother called. Benito thought she wanted him to quit playing, so he hid behind the garage and didn't answer.

"Benito, come here right away!" Mother called again. Benito's uncle wanted to take him to the lake, but he was in a hurry. Because Benito didn't come when he was called, he missed the trip. He was sorry he didn't come when Mother called.

When God calls people and they don't answer Him, they miss out on much more than a trip to the lake. They miss out on everything God wants to give them—faith, forgiveness, happiness, and life in heaven.

How does God call people? The apostle Paul says in our Bible verse, "[God] called you ... through our gospel." When ministers or Christian teachers or parents or anybody tells us that Jesus died for us and that God wants us to live with Him as His children, then God is calling us.

God is saying, "Benito! Ana! Ian! Please come and be one of My children. I have forgiven your sins because Jesus paid for them. I want you to have a home with Me in heaven and to enjoy My love on earth."

You'd think people would be glad to come when God calls, but many stay away from Him. They're afraid they may have to do something they don't want to do, or they think they have to stop having fun. But when they stay away from God, they miss the really great things they would enjoy—God's love and friendship.

We need God's love and forgiveness, His Holy Spirit, and His blessings. We want to live with Him in heaven. That is why we come when God's Holy Spirit calls us by the Gospel. The Gospel is the story of Jesus. The Gospel is God's promise of love. God is calling us to live with Him forever through the Good News that Jesus is our Savior.

Let's talk: Why didn't Benito come when his mother called? What did he miss? What does God want to give everyone? How does God call people to come to Him? Why don't all people come to God when He calls? How can we come to God and be with Him every day?

Older children and adults may read: Isaiah 55:1–7

Let's pray: Dear God, we thank You for calling us to enjoy all the good things You want to give to people. Please keep us from ever wanting to stay away from You. Give us Your love, through Jesus Christ, our Lord. Amen.

Remember your Creator in the days of your youth.
Ecclesiastes 12:1

They Were Never Babies

"Mom, why did God make Adam and Eve grown-up people?" asked Bryan. "Why didn't they have to be babies like everybody else?"

Before Mom could answer, Laurie did. "How could they be babies? God would have had to make some other adults to help Adam and Eve grow up," Laurie said.

Laurie was right. Babies need grown-ups. Most babies live with a father and a mother. Those who don't have their parents need someone else to love them and take care of them.

How will you become a good father or mother? Does it happen when you get married? No, right now you are becoming the kind of grown-up you will be. The kind of boy or girl you are now is the kind of man or woman you will probably be.

If you always get upset and angry when things go wrong, you'll probably be hard to live with when you are a father or mother. If you treat others with kindness, you'll probably be a kind parent who is fun to live with and helpful.

Ask God to help you control your temper and avoid rough actions, mean words, and selfishness. The Bible says, "Remember your Creator in the days of your youth." What you learn to do now is going to make you a better father or mother when you get married and have children.

And don't ever forget the way God has loved you and loves you every day. God loved us so much that He sent His Son to save us. Jesus loves you right now and He will love you when you are a grown-up too.

Let's talk: Which two people were never babies? Why didn't God make them babies? What kind of parents do babies need? How does a child grow up to be a good father or mother? How does your father or mother help you live with God in the days of your youth?

Older children and adults may read: Deuteronomy 6:4–7

Let's pray: Thank You, dear heavenly Father, for a Christian home with family devotions, prayers, and other ways of remembering You and staying close to You. Help us live with You now while we are young so that we can become good Christian parents when we grow up. We ask this for Jesus' sake. Amen.

Find out what pleases the Lord. Ephesians 5:10

What Pleases Jesus?

"Find out what your mother would like for her birthday, will you, Jenny?" said Mrs. Belz.

Jenny was a clever girl. She talked to her mother about many different things and never let her know why she was doing it. The next day, Jenny told Mrs. Belz her mother would like a new coffee maker.

"Thanks a lot, Jenny," said Mrs. Belz. "How did you find out?"

"Oh, I found out by getting her to talk to me. And then I listened," explained Jenny.

Some people say we can't find out what God would like from us. They think we can't know for sure what God wants and likes. But we can. We just have to do what Jenny did—listen. Jesus is God's Son, which means He is also God. We can learn to know God by listening to Jesus.

Jesus speaks to us in family devotions, in Bible readings, in Bible lessons, in church, and when we think about Him and have Him in our hearts. When we listen to what He tells us in His Word, we learn what our Lord Jesus wants.

The apostle Paul said, "Find out what pleases the Lord." We want to do that because God first loved us.

Let's talk: How did Jenny find out what her mother wanted for her birthday? How can we find out what pleases Jesus? When does Jesus speak to us? When do we speak to Him? What does the Bible verse tell us to try to learn? Why do God's children want to learn what pleases our Lord Jesus?

Older children and adults may read: Ephesians 5:8–14

Let's pray: Lord Jesus, please forgive us for often doing wrong and not doing what pleases You. Please help us to know what the will of God is and make us eager to do it. In Your name we pray. Amen.

How beautiful are the feet of those who bring good news!
Romans 10:15

The Best Kind of Doctor

The Wilson family was eating supper. Without anyone asking, Patrick said, "You know what I want to be when I grow up? I want to be a doctor."

"That's great," said Dad, rather surprised. "What made you decide to become a doctor?"

"Well, doctors make lots of money," answered Patrick.

"Is that the only reason you want to be a doctor?" asked Mom. "I thought people became doctors because they wanted to help others."

"Well, I guess that's a reason too," Patrick said. "I'll bet I could help people more by being a doctor than any other way."

"Did you know that one of the writers of the Bible was a doctor?" asked Dad.

"Really? Who?" asked Patrick.

"Dr. Luke," Dad answered. "The apostle Paul called Luke 'the beloved doctor.' Luke wrote the third book in the New Testament. He also wrote the book called 'The Acts of the Apostles.' "

"Do you think Luke became a doctor because he wanted to help people?" asked Patrick.

"I don't know," replied Dad. "But I'm sure he wanted to

help people after he knew Jesus. Luke helped their souls and their bodies."

"How'd he do that?" Patrick asked.

"He told people that Jesus was their Savior and Lord," explained Dad. "He taught them about Jesus—the Way to life with God."

"Do you think I could be that kind of doctor?" asked Patrick.

"There are nurses and doctors doing that kind of work today. We call them medical missionaries. They go to far-away countries to heal people with medicine and also to tell them the good news about Jesus. But you wouldn't make nearly as much money as a regular doctor," Dad told Patrick.

"That's all right. I'd like to be a medical missionary," Patrick said. "Then I could help their souls and their bodies. Telling people about Jesus would help them even more than medicine."

Let's talk: What was Patrick's first reason for wanting to become a doctor? What better reason did Mom give him?

What's the name of the doctor who wrote two books of the Bible? How did Dr. Luke help people? What do we call doctors who also tell people about Jesus? Have you ever talked to God about what you want to be when you grow up?

Older children and adults may read: Luke 10:1–9

Let's pray: Dear Jesus, no matter what I may become, teach me to serve You by helping others. And don't let me forget to help others especially by telling them about You. In Your name I pray. Amen.

Anyone who receives a prophet because he is a prophet will receive a prophet's reward. Matthew 10:41

How Pengo Became a Prophet

Pengo couldn't talk very well. In fact, most people couldn't understand him. When he was born, the top of his mouth wasn't right, and it never got any better.

Pengo lived in Africa. In his village there was only a witch doctor. The witch doctor couldn't help him. He just frightened Pengo by telling him that devils kept him from talking.

Then Pengo got smallpox. It left his face full of ugly scars. Soon after that his parents died, and nobody wanted Pengo. He had to live in a house all by himself.

One day a missionary came and told the people in Pengo's village about the love of Jesus. Pengo didn't have anyone who loved him, so he was excited to hear that Jesus loved him. Pengo began to love Jesus.

At first Pengo didn't tell anybody that he loved Jesus. He thought they would laugh. He only told Jesus. At night, when Pengo was alone, he would say, "I'm so glad You love me, Jesus. I'm so glad You died for me. I'm glad I belong to You now. I will find some way to show how much I love You."

So when the missionary needed a well, Pengo dug and carried away the dirt until the well was deep enough and there was water. When the missionary went on a trip, Pengo went along and helped. When new missionaries came, Pengo showed them where to go.

Pengo wished he could be a missionary, but missionaries have to talk, and Pengo still couldn't talk very well. But he did what he could, and it helped a lot.

Jesus has a surprise for Pengo. In heaven, Pengo will be counted as a missionary. Jesus said, "Anyone who receives a prophet because he is a prophet will receive a prophet's reward."

This means that what we do for God's workers counts the same as what the workers do. When we help a minister do God's work, that's the same as being a minister.

Let's talk: Who was Pengo? What problems did he have? How did Pengo learn about Jesus? What did he do for Jesus? Why did Pengo help the missionaries? What surprise will Jesus have for him? How can we get a prophet's reward?

Older children and adults may read: Matthew 10:38–42

Let's pray: Dear Jesus, we don't deserve any pay or reward for what we do for You, but we're glad You have promised great blessings to all who help Your servants. Please make us willing to help anyone we can help, but especially the pastors and teachers and missionaries who work for You. Amen.

Let us fix our eyes on Jesus ... who ... [suffered on] the cross. Hebrews 12:2 (RSV)

A Pretty Special Present

"Oh, boy! Today's my birthday," shouted Danielle as she got out of bed faster than usual.

Danielle could hardly wait to open her presents. That's because before she left for Europe, Danielle's aunt had promised to send her something very special for her birthday. The package had come yesterday!

Danielle tore the wrappings from her aunt's package first. But when she saw what was in the box, her mouth curled into a frown. "Aw, it's only an old wooden cross," she complained. "What good is that?"

Danielle's mother was sorry to hear what she said. "When we see a cross," Mom said, "it reminds us of what Jesus did for us—that He died for us on the cross. All who

believe that Jesus is their Savior receive the gift of life with God. That makes a cross something wonderful, doesn't it?"

Danielle was silent for awhile. Then she said, "I can put the cross in my bedroom and look at it while I say my prayers. It will help me remember that Jesus died for me and that I belong to Him."

Her mother was glad to hear what she said. The cross was a pretty special present after all.

"Let us fix our eyes on Jesus ... who ... [suffered on] the cross," says the Bible. The cross is a reminder of what Jesus has done for us.

Let's talk: What did Danielle get from her aunt for her birthday? Why didn't Danielle like it at first? What did Mom tell Danielle about the cross? Why does the Bible tell us to fix our eyes on Jesus?

Older children and adults may read: Matthew 10:37–42

Let's pray: Dear Lord Jesus, whenever I see a cross, may it remind me of how You suffered and died for me. Help me fix my eyes on You for forgiveness and life with God. Amen.

The gift of God is eternal life in Christ Jesus our Lord.
Romans 6:23

How Long Is Forever?

"Mother, how long is *forever?*" asked Ewaldo.

Mother thought for a moment. "It means always and always and always," she answered.

"That's the same as *eternal,* right, Mom?" said Lucena. She was older than Ewaldo and knew some big words.

"It is the same as *eternal,*" Mom said. "And the Bible tells us, 'The gift of God is eternal life in Christ Jesus our Lord.' Jesus gives us a life with God that will never end."

"Does that mean we'll be in heaven all the time when we die?" asked Lucena.

"Yes, and we have that life because Jesus came into our hearts," said Mom.

"But we're not in heaven yet," said Lucena. "Mrs. Cruz said heaven is a place where people go when they die."

Then Mom explained that heaven is living with Jesus forever. "Even though Jesus is in our hearts now, we can't see Him," Mom explained. "But when we die, we'll see Jesus just like we see each other right now. Jesus gives us eternal life with Him."

"Is eternal life the same as being in heaven?" asked Lucena.

"Yes," said Mom. "Now let's thank God for giving us this eternal life through Christ Jesus our Lord. The Bible says, 'Whoever believes in the Son [of God] *has* eternal life.' "

Let's talk: What does *forever* mean? What did Lucena say it means? When do people begin to have life with God? Why is heaven called eternal life? What did Lucena's mother want her to remember?

Older children and adults may read: Revelation 7:9–17

Let's pray: Thank You, God, for giving us eternal life through Jesus Christ our Lord. Keep us as Your children while we are living on earth. Then we will be with You in heaven forever after we die. We ask this in Jesus' name. Amen.

The wicked borrow and do not repay. Psalm 37:21

Borrowing and Keeping

"How about letting me use your knife?" Karl asked his friend Ian. "We're going camping this weekend, and I'll probably need one."

"Sure," agreed Ian. "But bring it back to me Monday 'cause I need it for our club meeting."

"I will," promised Karl. But when Ian asked Karl for his knife at school on Monday, Karl said he had forgotten to bring it.

Every day Ian asked Karl for his knife, and every day Karl said he forgot to bring it. Karl just didn't want to give the knife back.

On Friday, Ian went to Karl's house to make Karl give the knife back to him. He had to tell Karl's mother about the knife before Karl gave it back. After that Karl and Ian weren't friends anymore.

When someone is nice enough to lend us something, we need to remember that it's not ours "for keeps." When we're thankful for the loan, we return what we borrow as soon as possible. The Bible says, "The wicked borrow and do not repay."

It may not be easy to give something back that we like a lot, but God wants us to pay back what we borrow. It's not ours for keeps. Keeping is stealing. Stealing is a sin for which Jesus had to die. That's a pretty strong reminder to give back what we borrow.

Let's talk: What does God say about stealing? What causes some people to steal? What does the Bible call people who don't pay back what they borrow? How do we show we're

thankful that someone let us borrow something? Who helps us return what we borrow?

Older children and adults may read: Ephesians 4:28–30

Let's pray: Dear Jesus, please forgive the times we have wanted to steal or keep what didn't belong to us. You gave Your life for us. Help us resist the temptation to keep what isn't ours and instead gladly return what belongs to others. Amen.

God is love. 1 John 4:8

Who Loves a Homeless Person?

A man standing on a street corner handed Kimiko a piece of paper. On one side was the picture of a homeless person. The man hadn't shaved for a long time, there was food in his beard, his hair wasn't combed, his clothes did not match, and his shoes and pants were worn out.

Under the picture was the question "Who loves him?" On the other side were the words "Once he was his mother's darling son." And he probably was.

But who loves this homeless person now? As he walks down the street and begs for food and a place to stay, most people avoid him.

Who loves everyone—including homeless people? God does. The Bible says, "God is love." He showed His love by sending His Son, Jesus, to pay for our sins.

The Bible also says, "God loved the world." That includes every person who ever lived in it or who ever will live in it. "God so loved the world that He gave His one and only Son." In another place, the Bible says, "Jesus died for all."

Did Jesus die for homeless people too? Yes, He did. In fact, Jesus spent a lot of His time with persons that most people didn't want to be around—tax collectors, fishermen, and the poor.

That's the wonderful thing about God's love. We don't have to be rich or pretty or strong or important. We don't even have to be perfect. God loves us just as we are. God is love.

Let's talk: What was the picture on the paper handed to Kimiko? Who loves everyone—even homeless people? What did Jesus do for all people? What can we do for homeless people because God loves us? What's the best way to help those who don't know about Jesus?

Older children and adults may read: 1 John 4:7–11

Let's pray: Dear God, thank You for sending Jesus to save all people, not just the good or the great or the lovely. Please help us to be more loving, more kind, and more helpful to everyone. For Jesus' sake we ask this. Amen.

He will call upon Me, and I will answer him. Psalm 91:15

When God Said No

Every night at the end of her prayers, Mimi said, "And please, God, let me have a bike for my birthday."

But Mimi's mother didn't have a lot of money. Mother wanted to get Mimi a bike, but when her birthday came, she still didn't have enough money.

Mother worried that Mimi might not trust God anymore if she didn't get her bike. She had prayed so long and hard for a bike.

After Mimi opened her birthday presents, mother said, "Honey, I'm sorry you didn't get a bike. But don't blame God for not answering your prayers, I just didn't have enough money."

"God answered my prayers, Mom. He just said, 'No, not yet,' " Mimi said. "He'll give you the money when He wants me to have a bike."

Mother was happy that Mimi trusted God. She gave Mimi a big hug. Mimi had taught her mother an important lesson about prayer.

Mimi can teach us something about prayer too. God doesn't always say yes to our prayers. Some of the things we pray for might not be good for us. Because God loves us, He doesn't give us the things that may harm us.

God has three answers to prayers: yes, no, and wait.

God knows the best answer for us. Like Mimi, we must trust that He loves us even when He says no or not yet.

God always listens to His children's prayers, and in the Bible, He promises, "I will answer."

Let's talk: What did Mimi pray for every night before her birthday? Why was Mother worried? What did Mimi teach her mother about prayer? What does God promise to do when His children pray to Him? Why isn't His answer always yes?

Older children and adults may read: Psalm 91:14–16

Let's pray: Dear Father in heaven, help us trust You as Mimi did. Help us believe that You always answer Your children when they pray to You. Teach us to be happy even when You say no or not yet. We know You always love us. In Jesus' name we pray. Amen.

Better a little with the fear of the LORD than great wealth with [trouble]. Proverbs 15:16

When a Little Is Better than a Lot

Once there was a mouse who lived in the country. It wasn't always easy to find enough to eat. But there were no mousetraps in the field where the country mouse lived, so he was pretty safe.

One day the country mouse visited his cousin in the city. While he was there, the city mouse showed him all the food in his house. On the table, there was cheese, butter, sausage, and other foods that mice simply love to nibble at.

"I'd like to be a city mouse," said the country cousin. Just then a cat came into the room.

"Hurry, run for the hole," cried the city mouse. So they both ran for their lives. But in his hurry, the city mouse ran right into a mousetrap. *Whang!* He was dead.

The country mouse got into the hole before the cat caught him. As soon as he caught his breath, he left the house with all the good food and went back to the country. "I'd rather be safe than rich," he said.

Sometimes even Christians get jealous of people who have a lot of money. But this is foolish. The Bible says it is "better to have a little with the fear of the LORD than great wealth with [trouble]."

Jesus warned people about wanting to get rich. People who love money and lots of things often forget God. They easily lose their life with Him. The apostle Paul wrote: "People who want to get rich fall into temptation and a trap and into many foolish and harmful desires."

The worst trouble anyone could have would come from losing life with Jesus. To have only a little money or a few things and Jesus is much better than to be rich or famous without having His love and life with Him.

$$\approx$$

Let's talk: Where did the country mouse go for a visit? What happened to the rich city mouse? What did the poor country mouse decide? Why did Jesus warn us about wanting to get rich? What does our Bible verse say is better, a little with the Lord or a lot without Him?

Older children and adults may read: Luke 12:15–21

Let's pray: Dear Father in heaven, You know what we need and what is best for us. Please give us only what is good and what we can use to help others. Keep us from wanting great riches without You. Remind us that it's much better to have a little and life with You than great riches with trouble. In Jesus' name we ask this. Amen.

If you believe, you will receive whatever you ask for in prayer. Matthew 21:22

Learning to Pray

"Daddy! Daddy!" cried Deron as he ran up the front sidewalk. Dad hurried to the door and took the sobbing boy in his arms.

"What's the matter?" he asked.

"Oh, Daddy! Kelessie is awfully sick. An ambulance came and took her to the hospital," sobbed Deron. "Do you think she's going to die? Kelessie's my best friend, and I don't want her to die."

Then Deron began to cry even harder. Dad tried to think of some way to comfort him. "Isn't there anything we can do?" asked Deron.

Then Dad thought of a way to help. "You know, there is something we can do for Kelessie. We can pray," Dad said. "We can ask our Father in heaven to make Kelessie better. God loves her very much and knows what's best for her."

"Please pray to God right now, Dad," begged Deron.

But Dad said, "Since Kelessie is your best friend, don't you think you should be the one to ask God to help her?"

"What can I say?" asked Deron.

"Just tell God what's wrong, like you just told me. Ask Him to help," explained Dad.

So Deron prayed. "Dear God," he said, "Kelessie, my best friend, is really sick. I don't want her to die. Please make her well. Please do it for Jesus' sake. Amen."

After that, Deron felt a lot better, and so did his dad. They believed that God would do what was best for Kelessie.

God loves us and will always answer our prayers. We need to trust that He will answer us in the way that is best for us. Jesus said, "If you believe, you will receive whatever you ask for in prayer."

Let's talk: What did Dad tell Deron he could do for Kelessie? Why did Deron feel better after he prayed? What does it mean to have faith? What did Jesus promise to all who trust Him? How do we know that God loves us and will do what's best for us?

Older children and adults may read: John 15:13–16

Let's pray: Dear Jesus, please remind us to pray for whatever we need or want. Also teach us to believe that whatever we ask in Your name we will receive. Amen.

The cheerful heart has a continual feast. Proverbs 15:15

The Secret of a Good Life

"There goes Asad, happy as ever," said Stephanie. "He's always cheerful. Nothing seems to bother him."

"What makes you think nothing bothers him?" Stephanie's father asked.

"Well, when we let Asad play with us, he's happy. When we say he can't play, he says that he'll watch," explained Stephanie. "When someone calls him a name, Asad just smiles and doesn't mind at all."

"Maybe he knows the secret of how to be happy," said Dad.

"I wish I could be that way," replied Stephanie. Her feelings were hurt pretty easily.

"You can be that way if you do what Asad does," said Dad.

"What does he do?" asked Stephanie.

"Asad believes that God is always good to him," Dad said. "He's thankful for what he gets from God and doesn't complain."

"So Asad carries his fun around inside of him," said Stephanie. "I'm going to ask God to make me that way."

"That's a great idea," said Dad. "The Bible tells us that the person with a cheerful heart has a good life. We can always have a cheerful heart because Jesus loves us and has made us God's children."

Let's talk: Why was Asad always cheerful? What did Stephanie decide to ask God? How did God show that He loves us? How can we have a cheerful heart? Why can we always be happy with Jesus? Memorize the Bible verse.

Older children and adults may read: Psalm 103:1–13

Let's pray: Lord God, help us to be thankful that we have You as our Father and Jesus as our Savior. Give us the Holy Spirit so that we will always be cheerful. We ask this for Jesus' sake. Amen.

You help us by your prayers. 2 Corinthians 1:11

Each Night at Six

"We wish we could go with you," some of the young people told the missionary who had talked to their Sunday school. The missionary was leaving to work for Jesus in a country far away.

"Come with me in your prayers every day," said the missionary. "You can help me by praying for me."

"We could all promise to pray for you every evening at six o'clock," said Tiffany. And that's what some of them decided to do. Each night at six o'clock, they prayed for the missionary and his work.

Our prayers do great things for the people who work for God. God gladly listens to those prayers. The Bible says, "The prayer of a righteous man is powerful and effective."

The apostle Paul wanted his friends to pray for him. When he wrote to them, he said, "You help us by your prayers. Then many will give thanks for the gracious favor granted us in answer to the prayers of many."

Our missionaries today also say, "You help us by prayer." Our pastors and our teachers in the church say, "You help us by prayer." All the other people who work for Jesus in His church say, "You help us by prayer."

We could write a list of people to pray for. It would help us remember missionaries and other servants of Jesus. Let's pray for these people each night. They are doing their work for us, and we can help them by our prayers.

Let's talk: How did the young people find out they could help the missionary? What did they decide to do? What reason did the apostle Paul give his friends for praying? Who are some of the people we could help by prayer?

Older children and adults may read: 2 Corinthians 1:8–11

Let's pray: Dear Father in heaven, please remind us to pray often for Your missionaries and other church workers. Today we ask You to bless especially (*name the people for whom you want to pray*) and their work for You. In Jesus' name we ask this. Amen.

Christ Jesus came into the world to save sinners.
1 Timothy 1:15

Our Lord's Big Job

"Momma, why don't pictures ever show Jesus smiling?" asked Norberto.

Momma thought for a moment. "Not all pictures show Jesus looking serious. I remember a picture of Jesus smil-

ing," she said. "He was listening to some children praise Him in the temple, and He was smiling."

"That was on my Sunday school lesson," said Norberto. "But why do most pictures of Jesus show Him looking real serious?"

"Well, did you ever notice how serious the rulers of countries usually look in their pictures?" Momma asked.

"Sure, that's because they have a big job to do," said Norberto.

His mother nodded and said, "That's right. And Jesus had a much bigger job to do than any president or king. Jesus had the work of saving the whole world from sin and from the punishment of sin. He even had to die to finish His work."

Norberto thought about this awhile. "I guess it's a good thing that Jesus looks serious in His pictures," he said. "They remind us of how important His work was."

"Yes," said Momma. "And let's not forget that He did it for us. The Bible says, 'Jesus came into the world to save sinners,' and that includes us. And do you know something else?"

"What?" asked Norberto.

"I'm sure Jesus smiled often when He was with His friends," Momma answered.

"I think so too," said Norberto. "Anyone who loves people smiles at them."

Let's talk: Why do most pictures of Jesus show Him looking serious? What does our Bible verse say Jesus came to do? Who are the sinners? What did Jesus do to save us? How are we saved from our sins? Why did Norberto think Jesus smiled often?

Older children and adults may read: 1 Timothy 2:1–6

Let's pray: Dear Jesus, thank You for coming into the world to save sinners. Thank You also for saving us by coming into our hearts. Make us kind and friendly to others, and give us a bright smile because we belong to You. Thank You for Your love that You give us every day. Amen.

Get rid of all bitterness, rage and anger, brawling and slander. Ephesians 4:31

Unkind Words

"That Kaitlyn! She's always getting hundreds on her tests. I'll bet she cheats," Daria complained to some of her friends. Soon everyone was whispering that Kaitlyn got good grades because she cheated.

Daria knew that Kaitlyn didn't cheat. She knew that Kaitlyn studied hard to get good grades. But Daria was jealous. Her mother was always asking why she couldn't be like Kaitlyn. Saying something bad about Kaitlyn was Daria's way of getting even with Kaitlyn.

Because of what Daria said, the girls in the class would not talk to Kaitlyn anymore. They gave her mean looks and said mean things about her. This made Kaitlyn sad. She didn't even want to go to school.

When Daria saw what her unkind words had done to Kaitlyn, she began to feel bad about it. She tried to tell the other girls that Kaitlyn didn't really cheat. But some of the girls kept saying bad things about Kaitlyn.

At last Kaitlyn's parents decided that she should go to a different school. She just wasn't happy anymore because her feelings were hurt by the mean words. They moved to a different part of town. And all of this happened because one person was jealous and told a lie.

When you are tempted to say mean things about someone, remember God's commandment not to give false witness against our neighbor. Do you know what that means?

Martin Luther explained it this way: We should love God so much that we won't purposely tell lies about people. We won't mention their mistakes or talk about them behind their backs. We won't spread harmful stories about people. We will defend our neighbors and say the best we can about them.

Jesus died to take away our sins of unkind words. To His children, He says, "Get rid of all bitterness, rage and anger, brawling and slander."

Let's talk: What lie did Daria tell about Kaitlyn? Why was this wrong? What harm did Daria's words do? Can you say

God's commandment against lying? What does this commandment mean? What does our Bible verse say about evil words?

Older children and adults may read: 1 Peter 3:10–12

Let's pray: Dear Jesus, please take away all evil words from our mouths. Give us the Holy Spirit so that we will speak only what is good and helpful to others. Amen.

Give ... to God what is God's. Mark 12:17

Don't Steal from God

Nikki and Chelsea saw Brooke on the back steps of her house. She was playing with a beautiful doll. She was dressing it first in one pretty outfit and then in another.

"Can we play with you?" asked Nikki and Chelsea. Brooke was excited and said they could. But Chelsea and Nikki took the doll and the clothes and wouldn't let Brooke have them back. It made her cry, but they still wouldn't give the doll back.

What do you think of Nikki and Chelsea? They weren't fair to Brooke, were they?

Some people treat God that way. They take God's things and act as though His things belong to them. They use His gifts just for themselves and don't give anything back to God.

What belongs to God? Well, everything does. Our life comes from God and belongs to Him. Our time, our money, our family, our home, our mind—all our blessings are given to us by God. He wants us to use them to help other people.

Mr. Anders believed that everything he had really

belonged to God. He knew God was just letting him use His things for awhile. He also loved God for sending His Son, Jesus, to die for him. So Mr. Anders worked for God and gave God a part of all the money he received. He also used his car to take people to Sunday school and church. He spent time with God every day.

Do you know what God wants from us more than anything else? He wants our heart and our love. Jesus said the first commandment is "Love the Lord your God with all your heart and with all your soul and with all your mind and with all your strength." The more we do this, the easier it will be to give God the things that are God's.

Let's talk: Why was it wrong for Nikki and Chelsea to play with the doll by themselves? What things do we have that belong to God? How do some people take God's things

away from Him? How did Mr. Anders use his car for God? What does God want more than anything else? Why do Christians give things back to God?

Older children and adults may read: Malachi 3:7–10

Let's pray: Dear God, we thank You for the many things You have given us to use for awhile. Please help us remember that they really belong to You so that we will use them in Your ways and for Your work. In Jesus' name we ask this. Amen.

Let your light shine before men that they may see your good deeds and praise your Father in heaven. Matthew 5:16

Where Good Baby-sitters Come From

"Those baby-sitters from Grace Church are the best you can get," Mrs. Brant told Mrs. Grey. "Last night we had our third baby-sitter—and they're all wonderful."

"Who are they?" asked Mrs. Grey.

"Oh, they're a club of teenagers who took baby-sitting lessons at the church. They try to do their job for God as well as they can," explained Mrs. Brant. "They're kind, and they play well with the children. They tell Bible stories. They remind the children to pray, and they teach the children good behavior."

"I know my children need that," said Mrs. Grey.

"Our children love them," said Mrs. Brant. "I wouldn't get anyone else. These young people are well-behaved and honest. You can tell they love God in what they do. They aren't just trying to earn money."

"They certainly are letting their faith shine," commented Mrs. Grey.

"Yes, they are," agreed Mrs. Brant. "I hope my children will grow up with God in their hearts. It's wonderful what God can do to any person who loves Jesus."

Those two mothers were praising God for what those teenage baby-sitters did. Jesus wants us all to follow His teachings so that our words and actions will show those around us how wonderful God is. That's why He said, "Let your light shine before men that they may see your good deeds and praise your Father in heaven."

When we do and say things that show our love of Jesus, then people can see how God can change a person through His love. This may lead others to faith in Jesus so that they too can be God's children. So let your light shine.

Let's talk: Why did Mrs. Brant like the baby-sitters from Grace Church? What helped them do their job well? Why did Mrs. Grey praise God? What did Jesus say we should let

135

people see? Why? What is our light? How can we let our light shine?

Older children and adults may read: Matthew 5:13–16

Let's pray: Dear Father in heaven, please help us let the light of our love of Jesus shine in whatever we do. Make us more loving, more helpful, and more kind so that people will praise You for what we do. We ask this in Jesus' name. Amen.

Children, obey your parents in everything. Colossians 3:20

Who Knows What's Best?

"Aw, Mom, why can't I go over to Greg's house?" asked William.

"You know Greg is always getting into trouble," Mom answered.

"He never does anything bad when I'm with him," William argued. "Please, Mom, Greg's really okay. Why can't I go?"

"I'm sorry, William, but I think it would be better if you didn't go over to Greg's house," Mom said. "I've tried to explain why. You'll have to believe that I know what's best."

But William thought he knew better. He was very angry, and he even refused to eat supper. Instead, he just sat around grumbling. "My mom's so old-fashioned," he said. "Greg's a great guy. I'll bet I'm missing all kinds of fun tonight."

Later that evening the telephone rang. It was William's friend Nick. "Hey, did you hear what happened to Greg tonight?" Nick asked. "He got caught shoplifting."

As William hung up the phone, he told his mom what happened. "Wow! Greg's in jail. Am I ever glad I wasn't with him tonight!" William said. "Lucky for me you made me stay home. Thanks, Mom!"

William had learned that parents usually do know what's best.

In the Bible, God says, "Children, obey your parents in everything, for this pleases the Lord." God knows what's best. He wants His children to obey their parents. Those who do so out of love for Jesus please Him.

Let's talk: Why did William grumble and refuse to eat his supper? How did William learn that his mother was right? What does God say about children obeying parents? Why are Christian children willing to obey their parents? Memorize the Bible verse.

Older children and adults may read: Proverbs 1:7–15

Let's pray: Lord Jesus, teach me to gladly obey my parents, especially in all things that are pleasing to You. Amen.

You dishonor God by breaking the law. Romans 2:23

Wearing the Uniform of Christ

Julian's dad was admiring his son's new jacket. It had the name of their church across the back. Julian was on the church's basketball team.

"Mr. Evans told us to take off the jacket when we don't act like a Christian," said Julian. Mr. Evans was the team's coach. He wanted to be sure that the team didn't disgrace God or His church.

"I think that's a good idea," Dad said. "If people see you do something wrong in your church uniform, they might think less of God."

And that's true. The Bible says that breaking God's law dishonors God. In a way, Christians wear God's uniform as long as they call themselves Christians. When Christians do things, people don't just say, "Look at what they're doing." They often say, "That's how Christians act." If you do something that breaks one of God's laws, those around you may wonder if you're really a Christian. They may even think that God permits sin.

But when we're honest and polite and friendly and helpful and cheerful, people see that too. They may not only say, "Mari is the nicest girl," they'll also say,

"Christians act differently. I wonder why. I'd like to be one."

People who love God don't want to dishonor and disgrace Him by breaking His laws. Jesus has promised to help us avoid sin. And He gives us the Holy Spirit to guide our actions and make us children God can be proud of.

⁀

Let's talk: What kind of jacket was Julian wearing? When did Mr. Evans tell him to take off the jacket? What does the Bible say happens when God's children break His laws? What are some of His laws? How does Jesus help His people?

Older children and adults may read: Romans 2:21–24

Let's pray: Heavenly Father, please forgive us for Jesus' sake if we have shamed You before others. Give us the Holy Spirit so that Your name will be honored in all that we do. In Jesus' name we ask this. Amen.

Ask and it will be given to you. Matthew 7:7

A Right Way to Ask

"Bread!" shouted Ryley. But nobody at the table paid any attention to him. Before supper, Ryley's family had decided to teach him to say "please."

"Bread!" Ryley said a little louder. But nobody passed the bread.

"Bread!" he yelled. But Ryley still didn't get any bread.

"Will somebody *please* give me a piece of bread?" Ryley finally asked politely. Everybody tried to give him bread at the same time.

"Oh, I get it!" Ryley said. "You're trying to teach me to say 'please.' " He had found out that saying "please" works much better than shouting and demanding.

God, too, likes to be asked instead of told. When people get angry because God doesn't give them what they want, they forget that they deserve nothing but punishment from God because of their sin.

"Ask and it will be given to you," Jesus said. But Jesus also said when we pray, we must believe God and ask in a right Spirit. "If you believe, you will receive whatever you ask for in prayer," Jesus said.

What does it mean to believe? It means trusting that God loves us for Jesus' sake and that He is our Father. It means trusting that God is almighty and can answer any prayer. It means trusting that God is good and wants to give us only what's best for us. To have faith or believe in God is to trust God.

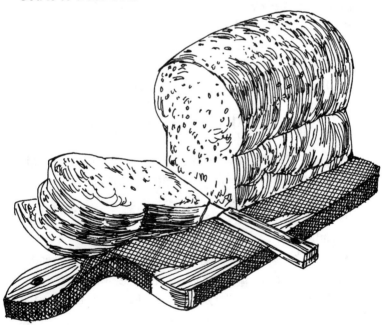

People who believe in God will ask Him for many things. And when we ask, we can trust that God hears our prayers and will answer.

Let's talk: Why didn't Ryley get the bread he wanted? What did he learn from his family? What did Jesus say about asking God for things? What are some wrong ways of asking? What does it mean to believe? How are we to ask God for things?

Older children and adults may read: Luke 11:5–13

Let's pray: Dear Father in heaven, please give us the Holy Spirit so that we will ask You for the things You want us to have in a right way. In Jesus' name we pray. Amen.

Everyone who competes in the games goes into strict training. 1 Corinthians 9:25

How to Be a Good Athlete

"Jerrold Higgins is the fastest runner in the world," Kent said at the supper table. "He never smokes or drinks. He doesn't even drink coffee!"

"And he always gets plenty of sleep," said his mother, because Kent never wanted to go to bed.

"I want to be a good athlete if I can't be a minister," said Kent.

"To be a good athlete you have to practice every day," said Dad.

"Sure, it's like playing the piano," said Kent's sister, Catherine. "Sometimes I get so tired of practicing. But now I like it better because I can play hard songs."

"It takes hard work to be good in anything," said Mother. "Even Christians need to practice."

"Pastor talked about that at church," said Kent. "The apostle Paul told us to be sure to win our race. He meant our race to heaven."

"That's right," said Dad. "And do you remember what Paul said every good athlete does? 'Everyone who competes in the games goes into strict training.' What do you think that means?"

Kent thought it meant being in good physical shape. "You're right," said Dad. "But Paul told us that athletes train to win a prize that isn't worth much; we train for God."

"But that's much more than taking care of our bodies," Mom added. "It also means training ourselves to do what God wants, such as helping others, praying, going to church, and saying no to sin."

"Wow! That's a lot to practice!" said Kent.

"It certainly is," agreed Mother. "But God's Holy Spirit helps us practice and makes us strong Christians so we can win our race to heaven."

Let's talk: How did Jerrold Higgins keep himself strong? Why did he do this? What did the apostle Paul say every good athlete does? How does God help us win our race to heaven?

Older children and adults may read: 1 Corinthians 9:24–27

Let's pray: Heavenly Father, please help us avoid everything that might make us lose the race to heaven. Lead us to do those things that will bring us safely to You in heaven. We ask this in the name of Jesus, who died to save us. Amen.

[God said], "This is My Son, whom I love. Listen to Him!"
Mark 9:7

Better Listen to Jesus

"Better take your raincoat along, Orlanda," said Mother. "It looks like rain."

"Come on, Mom, you're always afraid it's going to rain," complained Orlanda. "It won't rain."

When Orlanda came home, she was soaked to the skin, and she was shivering. She caught such a bad cold that she missed three days of school, including her class party.

It would have been better if Orlanda had listened to her mother. God wants children to obey their parents. He has given them to us to help us grow up. Parents guide us in proper choices about how we act and talk as their children and, more importantly, as God's children.

But there is a worse kind of not listening. God the Father said several times in the Bible, "Jesus is My Son. Listen to Him." When people don't listen to Jesus, they get into trouble with God.

Jesus says He is our Savior. He said that all people are lost sinners and that He came to save them. He said He is the Good Shepherd, who gave His life for His sheep. People need to listen to His words.

Jesus also says in the Bible that we need His forgiveness every day because we sin every day. But some people don't believe Jesus. They think they're all right the way they are. They don't believe Jesus or follow Him.

Jesus said, "Come to Me, all you who [have worries and troubles], and I will give you rest." Jesus said this because He loves us and wants to help us. But many people don't listen.

Jesus wants us to obey His teachings. To His followers He said, "If anyone loves Me, he will obey My teaching. My Father will love him, and We will come to him and live with him."

God the Father wants us to listen to Jesus because Jesus saves us and blesses us. Through Jesus, we have God's forgiveness and love and a wonderful home in heaven. The more we listen to Jesus, the better.

Let's talk: What happened to Orlanda because she didn't listen to her mother? Who said that all people should listen to Jesus? Why should we listen to Jesus? What are some things Jesus said? What does Jesus give those who listen to Him? What happens when people don't listen to Jesus?

Older children and adults may read: Mark 9:2–7

Let's pray: Dear God, our Father in heaven, please make us willing to listen to Jesus at all times. Strengthen our faith in Jesus, our Savior. Bring us safely to heaven so that we can have the life You want to give us through Him. In Jesus' name we ask it. Amen.

You do not have, because you do not ask God. James 4:2

You Can Keep Asking God

Tomeo and Sumiko went to a skating rink with two friends. But the rink was closed. A man who was sweeping the entrance told them it wouldn't be open until tomorrow.

Sumiko and Tomeo hung around awhile longer, but their friends went home. "How about letting us skate just a little while?" Sumiko asked the man. "We'll try not to get in your way if you'll let us in."

"Well, all right," said the man. So Tomeo and Sumiko

got in because they asked. Their friends missed out on skating.

God wants us to ask Him for what we want. Even if it's something we think we can never have, God wants us to ask for it. He says, "You do not have, because you do not ask Me." In another place, Jesus said, "Ask and it will be given to you." God will give us those things that we need and that are good for us.

God even wants us to *keep* asking if our prayers aren't answered right away. It isn't right to whine and pout for things, but God wants us to keep asking Him for what we want or need.

Jesus told a story about a man who got some company late at night. The company was hungry, but he didn't have any food. So the man went to his neighbor's house to ask for some bread. He pounded on the door.

At first the neighbor said, "Don't bother me. My children and I are already in bed." But when the man kept asking, his neighbor got up and gave him what he wanted.

When Jesus finished telling this story, He said, "Everyone who asks receives; he who seeks finds; and to him who knocks, the door will be opened."

☙

Let's talk: How did Sumiko and Tomeo get into the skating rink? Why didn't their friends get in? What story did Jesus tell about asking? Why did Jesus tell that story? What does the Bible verse say? What does it teach us?

Older children and adults may read: Luke 11:5–10

Let's pray: Dear heavenly Father, we're glad that You want us to ask You for whatever we want. Please teach us to pray more than we do. Remind us of Your promise to give us what is good for us if we ask You for it. In Jesus' name we ask this. Amen.

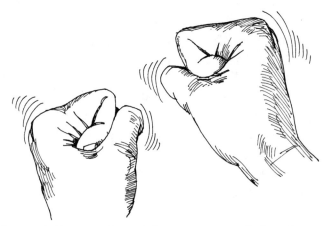

From within, out of men's hearts, come evil thoughts.
Mark 7:21

Where the Trouble Lies

One day when Dustin was home alone, he dropped the kitchen clock. When he picked it up, the hands wouldn't run right. He took the glass off and took the hands to the hardware store. There was a man there who could fix clocks.

"Please fix these hands right away," Dustin said to the clock repairman.

The man laughed. "The hands are all right," the man said. "If you want me to fix the clock, you'll have to bring me the *inside* of the clock."

"But it's the hands that aren't working," explained Dustin.

"I know," said the man. "But that's because there's something wrong *inside* the clock."

When *your* hands go wrong, do you know that the trouble is inside you? If your hands hit someone or steal or do other wrong things, putting medicine on your hands won't make them better.

To fix what your hands do, God has to fix your heart or spirit, which is on the inside of you. Jesus said, "From within, out of men's hearts, come evil thoughts." First we think wrong, and then we do wrong.

God fixes us on the inside by giving us the Holy Spirit. The Holy Spirit gives us a new heart, a heart that loves Jesus, our Savior, and wants to be like Him. God does this fixing free of charge. And because of Jesus, He forgives us when we sin. When He fixes us on the inside, our hands go right. In fact, our whole behavior gets straightened out.

⤦

Let's talk: What did Dustin want the clock repairman to do? Why couldn't the man fix the hands? When our hands go wrong, what needs fixing? What did Jesus say about this?

Older children and adults may read: Mark 7:14–23

Let's pray: Please give us a new, clean heart, O God, and a right spirit inside us. Forgive us our sins for Jesus' sake, and help us to think His way so that we will walk in His ways. In Jesus' name. Amen.

When I am weak, then I am strong. 2 Corinthians 12:10

Weak but Mighty

Pastor Jacobs asked Mr. Wyler to be a Sunday school teacher.

"But I can't teach," Mr. Wyler said. "I don't know my Bible well enough. I don't know how to handle children. You better get somebody else."

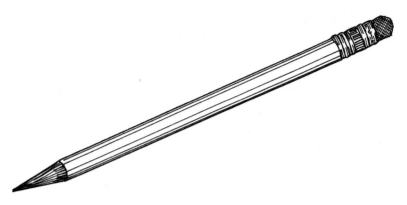

"What's this lying here?" asked Pastor Jacobs.

"A pencil," answered Mr. Wyler, wondering what Pastor Jacobs had in mind.

"What can a pencil do by itself?" asked Pastor Jacobs.

"It can't do anything by itself," said Mr. Wyler. He smiled as he began to see what was coming. "It depends on who holds the pencil and what he does with it."

"I see," said the pastor. "Are you like a pencil that hasn't been sharpened, or are you a pencil that God can't use?"

"Oh, I'm sure God could do something with me if He took hold of me," said Mr. Wyler, laughing at himself.

"Why don't you let Him use you as a teacher?" asked Pastor Jacobs. "The children in our Sunday school need teachers."

"But aren't there some better people God could use?" Mr. Wyler still argued.

"Perhaps," answered Pastor Jacobs, "but God told the apostle Paul, 'My power is made perfect in weakness.' That's why Paul said, 'For Christ's sake, I delight in weaknesses. ... For when I am weak, then I am strong.' Christians who know how weak they are, are the strongest when they ask God to make them strong."

Mr. Wyler decided to join the Sunday school teacher-training class. And when he asked God to help him become a good teacher, God made him strong.

≈

Let's talk: What was Mr. Wyler asked to do? Why didn't he want to? Who are the strongest Christians? Why are we strong only when we know we are weak? Why was the apostle Paul satisfied to be weak? What did Mr. Wyler decide to do?

Older children and adults may read: 2 Corinthians 12:7–10

Let's pray: Dear Lord, we're small and weak in Your kingdom, and we can do nothing without Your power. Help us remember that we're weak so that You can do great things through us. In Jesus' name we ask it. Amen.

A gentle answer turns away wrath. Proverbs 15:1

The Best Fighting System

Lita came home full of energy after school. Her last class had been P.E.

"We're learning self-defense," she said. "We're learning the Sullivan System."

"What's the Sullivan System?" Mother asked.

"It's hitting the other person before he can hurt you," answered Lita.

"What do you think of the *Solomon* System?" Mother asked.

"The *Solomon* System?" repeated Lita. "I've never heard of it."

"It's the best system in the world," said Mother.

"What's it like, Mom?" Lita asked.

"You'll find it in Proverbs 15:1," Mother answered, pointing to the Bible on the table.

"In the Bible?" Lita asked. But she picked up the book and found the verse. Lita read, "A gentle answer turns away wrath."

"I get it," said Lita. "Tyrell did that when Justin was mad and wanted to fight him."

"What did Tyrell say?" Mother asked.

"He said, 'I'm sorry, Justin, I'd rather be your friend,' " Lita said. "And it took the fight right out of Justin."

"Isn't that the easiest way to win a fight?" Mother asked. "That's the way Jesus won His fights with His enemies."

Let's talk: What was Lita learning in P.E.? What system did Solomon teach? Where did Lita find the Solomon System? Why is a gentle answer the best way to win a fight? How does Jesus help us give gentle answers?

Older children and adults may read: Proverbs 15:1–4

Let's pray: Father in heaven, we have such sharp tongues, and we're so quick to say mean things. Please forgive us. Make us more loving so we will give soft answers and win fights by making peace, as Jesus would. In His name we ask this. Amen.

If someone strikes you on the right cheek, turn to him the other also. Matthew 5:39

Why Not Hit Back?

"Charles, why did you push Anne?" his mother asked him sadly.

" 'Cause she pushed me first," Charles answered. He thought that meant he could push her back.

"What do you think Jesus would have done, Charles, if He had been pushed?" Mother asked.

"He would have—I don't know what He would have done," Charles responded.

"I know what He said about hitting back," Mother said. "Look at Matthew 5:39 in the Bible for the answer."

Charles got his Bible, and together they found the verse. In it Jesus said, "If someone strikes you on the right cheek, turn to him the other also."

"Does this mean Jesus would have said, 'You can push Me again?' " asked Charles.

"That's what it sounds like to me," agreed Mother. "At least He wouldn't have pushed back."

So, are God's children to let people push them and hit them? No, we need to protect ourselves. But Jesus meant that it's better to be hurt than to hurt somebody. He wants us to love even those who hurt us. And He would rather we let someone hurt us a second time than get angry and hit back.

Jesus let people hurt Him and even kill Him to save everyone from their sins. He saved us too. When Jesus is in our hearts, we can keep from hitting and hurting others even when they push us.

⤳

Let's talk: What did Anne do? How did Charles respond? Why did Charles think it was all right to push back? What do you think Jesus probably did when someone pushed Him? What did Jesus say about hitting back? Why can we willingly forgive people who hurt us? Who makes us willing?

Older children and adults may read: Matthew 5:38–42

Let's pray: Dear Father in heaven, we often get angry and want to hit back. Please forgive us for Jesus' sake. Help us to act as You want us to. In Jesus' name we ask this. Amen.

Whoever can be trusted with very little can also be trusted with much, and whoever is dishonest with very little will also be dishonest with much. Luke 16:10

What Small Things Tell

A business owner always watched his new workers carefully.

One day he hired a boy to sweep and clean in his factory. The business owner asked the boy's boss to let the boy word on his own, but report what the boy did with his time.

After a week, the boy's boss told the business owner, "The boy does his work well and takes good care of the things he works with."

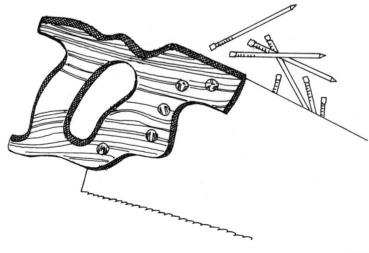

The owner was glad to hear this, but he decided to see for himself. Just before the boy started working, the owner threw a clean rag on the floor and laid a saw on some nails. Then he watched.

When the boy came by, he picked up the rag, shook it out, and laid it with his other clean rags. Then he picked up the saw and hung it on the wall where it belonged. He put the nails in the drawer where they belonged.

When the owner saw that the boy was careful in little things, he asked the boy, "How would you like a job in our office? If you will keep on doing your work well, we'll make you a manager someday."

This business owner could see that the boy would be a good worker. He could tell by watching how he did his little jobs. The little things we do, even when we are young, tell the story of how well we will probably do big things when we are older.

That's part of what Jesus meant when He said, "Whoever can be trusted with very little can also be trusted with much, and whoever is dishonest with very little will also be dishonest with much."

Let's talk: What did the business owner ask the factory boss to watch? Why did the owner throw a clean rag on the floor? How did the boy show he could be trusted to do his work well? How can people tell how we will act when we're older? Why do we want to do our work well?

Older children and adults may read: Luke 16:10–13

Let's pray: Heavenly Father, please help us do our work and even little things well so that we will grow up to be good workers for our Lord Jesus. In His name we ask this. Amen.

When tempted, no one should say, "God is tempting me."
James 1:13

The Moths That Got Burned

It was nighttime. Herschel and Tiana were watching a big moth flying around the porch light. The moth kept hitting its head against the hot glass. But that didn't stop the moth from flying at the light. It wanted to get in.

A few days later, Mother cleaned the porch light. When she took the shade off, about a dozen dead moths fell out. They had died trying to get into the light. The light had burned them.

"You know what this reminds me of?" Mother said to Herschel and Tiana, who were watching. "It reminds me of how we often want something that isn't good for us. Then we can get hurt because we follow our temptations."

"But a moth can't help wanting to get to the light, can it?" asked Herschel.

"Well, no," said Mother. "And in a way we're as helpless as a moth. We can't keep ourselves from being tempted to sin. The bad wishes are in us. But we can't blame God for that. He didn't make us that way. The Bible says, 'God doesn't tempt anyone, but each one is tempted by his own evil desire.' "

"But how can we keep from hurting ourselves when we're tempted like those foolish moths?" asked Tiana.

"That's a good question," said Mother. "God helps us fight our wrong wishes. He even gives us a new spirit. He puts His Holy Spirit inside us to guide our thoughts and actions."

"I get it," said Herschel. "God helps us get rid of wanting to sin."

"Now you see a light that won't hurt you," said Mother.

"God comes and lives in us through Jesus. Jesus makes us want what God wants because Jesus is God."

~

Let's talk: What happened to the moths that wanted to get into the porch light? Why didn't the moths quit flying at the light? What did Mother tell Herschel and Tiana as she cleaned the light? Why can't we blame God when we listen to temptations? How does God come into a person's heart?

Older children and adults may read: James 1:13–17

Let's pray: Dear Father in heaven, please forgive us and help us when we are tempted to sin. Give us the Holy Spirit so we won't follow temptations but will do what is right. This we ask for Jesus' sake. Amen.

By your words you will be [judged]. Matthew 12:37

We Are What We Say

April found out she could scare people. When she got real angry and said nasty words, the other children would quit teasing her. So April learned to say mean, nasty things, even though she believed in Jesus and knew He didn't want her to say them. April even thought she had a right to be hateful.

Her mother knew April needed help. She wanted her daughter to act more Christlike. One day Mother told April what Jesus had said about the words we speak.

"April," she said, "Jesus told His enemies: 'How can bad people like you say good things? The words of your mouth come from what's in your heart. The good man gives good things out of his good heart, and the evil man gives evil things out of his evil heart. In the day when God will judge people, you will be judged by your words.'

"You see," Mother continued, "we don't only talk the way we *are*, but we also *are* the way we talk. Because we belong to Jesus and are God's children, we want to be God's children, especially in the way we talk."

April agreed. And as April thought more about Jesus, she talked more about Him. And when she tried to please Him in what she said, she used kind words and hardly ever said anything mean or hateful.

Our words tell what kind of person we really are. Sometimes we can say nice things and not mean them, or we can say bad things and be sorry for them. But as Jesus said, before we know it, our words give us away. They are like the fruit on a tree. They show what kind of tree we are.

Let's talk: How do you think April felt in her heart when she said mean things? What did Jesus tell His enemies

about their words? What do you think they said about Him? What do people say about Jesus when they believe in Him? How does Jesus change our way of talking? What did Jesus mean when He told His enemies they would be judged by their words?

Older children and adults may read: Matthew 12:33–37

Let's pray: Dear Father in heaven, like April, we often say evil words because we are sinners, but we're sorry. Please forgive us for Jesus' sake. Help us show by all our words that we love You. In Jesus' name we pray. Amen.

In quietness and trust is your strength. Isaiah 30:15

Like Learning to Swim

"Learning to swim is like being a Christian," Alec told his swimming teacher.

"What do you mean?" asked the teacher.

"Well, you told us to throw ourselves into the water and not be afraid of it," Alec said. "You said it would hold us up if we wouldn't fight it."

"Yes, but how is that like being a Christian?" asked the teacher.

"To be a Christian, you have to trust God to hold you up. My pastor said you have to throw yourself into the arms of Jesus," explained Alec.

Alec was right. We Christians trust that Jesus is our Savior. We trust that He will help us. It's like a swimmer who trusts that the water will hold him up, or a child who trusts that Dad will catch her when she jumps.

A person who's afraid of water will never be a good swimmer. The person who doesn't trust God's love will never be a strong and happy child of God. But the person who calmly trusts God will be a strong Christian.

In the book of Isaiah, God says, "In quietness and trust is your strength." That means we are strong Christians when we quietly believe the promises of God. He has promised to love us through Jesus, our Savior. Quietly believe that and you will be strong.

Let's talk: What did Alec ask his swimming teacher? How is being a Christian like learning to swim? What must a person believe to be a Christian? What did God say will make us strong Christians? How does trusting in God's love help us to be strong and happy Christians?

Older children and adults may read: Psalm 71:1–5

Let's pray: Lord God, our Father in heaven, thank You for promising to give us Your love through our Savior Jesus. Give us the Holy Spirit so that we will quietly trust in Your love. Please make us strong and happy Christians through a quiet trust in Jesus. In His name we pray. Amen.

You have been set free from sin and have become slaves to God. Romans 6:22

Who Will Get You?

Carter's father wasn't a good man. He often came home drunk. Instead of teaching Carter to love God, his father used God's name to say mean things.

Carter's mother tried to teach her son and take care of him by herself. One day Alicia asked if Carter could go to Sunday school with her. His mother said yes.

A few Sundays later, Carter arrived at Sunday school early, and so did his teacher, Mr. Ritter.

"Carter, what do you think you'll be when you grow up?" asked Mr. Ritter.

"That depends on who gets me," answered Carter.

Mr. Ritter was rather puzzled. "What do you mean?" he asked.

"Well, if the devil gets me, I may be a drunk, like my father. If God gets me, maybe I'll be a minister," Carter explained.

"You're a wise young man," said Mr. Ritter. "I believe God already has you, and He won't let you go. He's very happy that you're one of His children."

The Bible says we belong to whomever we obey. When we sin, then we are slaves of sin, and the devil has us in his power. When we obey God, then we are His servants, and God is in control of our lives.

That's why the apostle Paul said to Christians, "Thanks be to God that, though you used to be slaves to sin ... you have become slaves to righteousness. ... You have been set free from sin and have become slaves to God."

How does this happen? It happens when the Holy Spirit works faith in our hearts. Then we believe that Jesus died for our sins. Jesus sets people free from sin and makes them servants of God. That's why it's so important to belong to Him.

Let's talk: What did Mr. Ritter ask Carter? What did Carter say? What did Carter think he might be if God got him? Who has us in his power when we sin? Who sets people free from sin? How do we show that we belong to God?

Older children and adults may read: Romans 6:16–23

Let's pray: Lord Jesus, we thank You for setting us free from sin. We're glad that we belong to God. Please help us learn what You want us to do, and make us willing and able to do it for Your sake. Amen.

Come near to God and He will come near to you.
James 4:8

How Far Away Is God?

"Daddy, is God way up there where the airplane is?" asked little Risa.

"He sure is, honey," Dad said.

"And when it flies far away, is God where the airplane is then?" Risa asked.

"Yes, God is there too," Dad answered.

"Is God always far away?" asked Risa.

"No," replied Dad. "God is everywhere, and He's also very close to us."

"How can I be real close to God?" asked Risa.

"There's a Bible verse that tells you," Dad said. "It says, 'Come near to God and He will come near to you.' "

"But how can I come near to God?" she asked.

"That's not hard," answered Dad. "All you have to do is listen to what God says in the Bible and think about what He's done for you and what He wants you to do. You come near to Him every time you pray."

"You mean all I have to do is think about God and talk to Him?" asked Risa.

"Yes," said Dad. "When you believe that God loves you, then God is very close to you."

"I believe that," said Risa. "I know that Jesus died for me. He wouldn't have done that if He didn't love me."

Let's talk: What did Risa ask her dad? What did he tell her? Where is God? What Bible verse did Dad teach Risa? When do we come near to God? Why was Risa sure that God loved her?

Older children and adults may read: Genesis 28:10–16

Let's pray: Heavenly Father, thank You for coming near to us even before we come to You. Thank You for loving us for Jesus' sake. Help us come near to You every day through our prayers and devotions. In Jesus' name we pray. Amen.

As high as the heavens are above the earth, so great is His love. Psalm 103:11

No End to God's Love

"I wish I could jump as high as a telephone pole," said Myron.

"I wish I could jump as high as our hotel," said Ross.

"I wish I could jump as high as the Empire State Building," said Gina. "That's one of the highest in the world."

"I wish I could jump as high as the sky," Ross said.

"There's nothing that high," said Myron.

"Oh, yes, there is," said his dad, who had been listening. "If you'll look up Psalm 103:11, you'll find something that's as high as the sky is above the earth."

Myron and Ross raced to get their Bibles. When they found the verse, Myron gave the Bible to Gina to read it. " 'As high as the heavens are above the earth, so great is His love for those who fear Him.' How can you pile up love?" Gina asked.

"You can't pile up love. I don't get it," agreed Ross.

"God wants to tell us there is no end to His love, Ross," said Dad. "God's love goes on and on for those who trust that Jesus is their Savior. That's why the Bible says, 'As high as the heavens are above the earth, so great is His love.' "

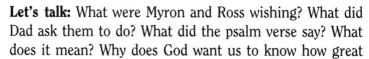

Let's talk: What were Myron and Ross wishing? What did Dad ask them to do? What did the psalm verse say? What does it mean? Why does God want us to know how great His love is?

Older children and adults may read: Psalm 103:8–12

Let's pray: Dear Father in heaven, how terrible it would be if Your love ended! Because we sin so much, we need so much love. We're glad that Your love is higher than the sky and deeper than the ocean. Please keep us happy in Your great love for the sake of Jesus, our Savior. Amen.

The LORD detests all the proud of heart. Proverbs 16:5

Pete's Trouble

"I'm the best player on the baseball team. Out of the way, Shrimp; let a *man* go by," said Kellan as he pushed Zack out of his way.

It was hard to like Kellan. He always acted as if he owned the team and the field and the school and everything else in the world.

"Did I tell you how I hit two homers in one game?" Kellan would say loudly when a group of kids gathered. Even if they were talking about something else, Kellan would start bragging about himself.

When Kellan noticed that he didn't have any friends, he tried to blame others. "They're all jealous," he said. "They know I'm the best ballplayer and the best wrestler and an all-around champion. That's why all these shrimps hate me."

It wasn't long before most of the children were disgusted with Kellan. Even God gets disgusted with people who are proud and think they're the best. The Bible says, "The LORD detests all the proud of heart."

When we act proud in front of God, we look really foolish because we make many mistakes. We're never as good as God wants us to be. We're sinners. And God hates sin.

So it's foolish to think we are the best. We need to say every day, "Dear God, please forgive our sins for Jesus' sake and help us do better." Then God forgives us, even if we've been proud. God looks at Jesus' perfect life instead of our sinful one. Then God gives us something we can be very proud of—He makes us His children.

Let's talk: Why did Kellan lose all his friends? Why did Kellan brag? How does God feel about proud people? Why is it foolish to think we're good? How do we receive forgiveness from God?

Older children and adults may read: Luke 18:9–14

Let's pray: Dear Father in heaven, please forgive all the proud thoughts we have about ourselves. Love us for Jesus' sake, and give us the Holy Spirit so that we will admit our faults and depend on You. In Jesus' name we ask it. Amen.

How can a young man keep his way pure? By living according to Your Word. Psalm 119:9

When to Cut Thistles

On the Lemp farm there was a big patch of thistles near the house. Thistles are weeds that have sharp points on them. One day Natalie told her father, "Today I'm going to cut down those thistles in our yard."

"That's great, Natalie," said Dad. "You promised to do it long ago. I'm glad you're finally getting around to it."

So Natalie cut down the thistles. She got so many scratches from them that her arms started to bleed. Natalie's mother helped her clean the scratches and put on Band-Aids.

A few weeks later, Dad was working in the yard. "You know, Natalie, this is how I would cut those thistles from now on," Dad said. And he took a hoe and quickly chopped off the new thistles that were growing. "See? Not even a scratch."

"Sure, but they were a lot smaller than the ones I had to cut," said Natalie.

"You should have cut the thistles when they were just starting to grow," explained Dad. "Did you know there are other kinds of weeds that can hurt you more than thistles? Your quick temper is a sharp weed, and your teasing, and even when you don't do things you should. These are all thistles that can hurt your life. You need to cut them before they get too big."

In Psalm 119, the writer asked himself a question. He said, "How can a young man keep his way pure?" How can he keep the thorns and thistles of sin from growing in his life?

Weeds grow in every garden. No one can get rid of all of them. But we can dig them up or cut them down. And they're easier to get rid of when they're just starting to grow.

In the same way, sins are like weeds in the garden of our heart. When we ask God to take away our sins for Jesus' sake, He plows them up. But even in a plowed field they keep popping up. So we need to ask God to help us cut them as soon as we notice them.

"How can a young man keep his way pure? By living according to Your Word," says the Bible. God's Word points out the weeds we need to cut before they grow and hurt us.

⁀

Let's talk: Why did the thistles hurt Natalie? What did Dad show Natalie? What's usually the best way to get rid of weeds? How does Jesus take away the weeds of sin in our hearts? How does He help us keep the thistles of sin from growing in our lives?

Older children and adults may read: Proverbs 3:1–7

Let's pray: Dear Jesus, please take away all my sins and give me a new, clean heart every day. When the thorns of sin begin to grow in my life, help me cut them out at once before they grow and become hard to get rid of. Amen.

I desire to depart and be with Christ, ... but it is more necessary for you that I remain in the body. Philippians 1:23–24

A Good Reason for Living

Once there was a young man whose nose was much longer than most people's. Almost every day, somebody teased him about his nose. When he looked at himself in the mirror, he didn't think anyone would ever like him. He wanted to kill himself.

Did he have to die? No, God wanted him to live. In fact, God commands, "You shall not kill." This includes killing yourself.

The man couldn't change his nose, but he could have changed the way he acted so others would want to be around him. An inventor named Steinmetz had a disfig-

ured body, but he made many wonderful things that made life better for others. Abraham Lincoln wasn't a beautiful person on the outside, but people admire him for his actions to free the Southern slaves.

The apostle Paul had a good reason for wanting to die. He said, "I wish I could die and be with Christ." But did he kill himself? No, he knew that would be wrong. He knew God had work for him to do here on earth. He said, "To go on living is more necessary."

That's what the man with the long nose said. "I'll use my life for God. I'll help others. I'll tell others about Jesus and His love. I'll live for Jesus as long as He lets me."

Jesus has wonderful plans for each one of us. He has a lot of work for us to do. Even though it will be wonderful to be with Him in heaven, it's necessary for us to live on earth as long as He wants us to.

Let's talk: Why did the young man want to die? Why is it wrong to want to die? Why did the apostle Paul want to die? What did he say was more necessary? When are we ready to die? What good reason do we have for living?

Older children and adults may read: Philippians 1:20–26

Let's pray: Father in heaven, we know that You made us for a good reason. We pray that You will show us what You want us to do in this world. Please keep us from ever wanting to stop living. Make us willing to serve You until You are ready to take us to heaven. In Jesus' name we pray this. Amen.

Love your neighbor as yourself. Leviticus 19:18

How to Love Others

"Somebody ought to tell Mr. Baxter that his son steals," said Mikhal.

"I'm not going to be the one," said Elana. "That's just asking for trouble."

Mikhal and Elana didn't tell Mr. Baxter. And his son kept stealing. One day the police caught him stealing a car, and he was sent to jail.

Wouldn't it have been better if Mikhal and Elana had talked to Mr. Baxter? Maybe they could have helped his son before it was too late.

In the Old Testament, God said, "Love your neighbor as yourself." When Jesus lived on earth, He said, "The most important commandment is this, 'Love the Lord your God with all your heart and with all your soul and with all your mind and with all your strength.' The second is this, 'Love your neighbor as yourself.' There is no commandment greater than these."

What does it mean to love your neighbor as yourself? Jesus put this law of God in another way. He said, "What you want others to do to you, do that to them." We call this the Golden Rule.

If you were Mr. Baxter, would you want someone to tell you about your son's stealing? Would you want others to keep you out of trouble or help you when you're in trouble? Yes, of course.

This doesn't mean we should "butt into" other people's business. But when we can keep someone from getting into trouble or when we can help someone, God wants us to do so. "Love your neighbor as yourself."

And "neighbor" doesn't only mean people who live next door to us. It means anybody.

We don't always love other people the way we love ourselves. That's why Jesus had to save us. But Jesus makes us willing and able to love others. Ask Him to help you love others as you love yourself.

Let's talk: Why didn't Elana want to tell Mr. Baxter that his son was stealing? Why should she have told? How much did God say we are to love our neighbor? Who is our neighbor? How important did Jesus say this commandment is? What do we need from God because we don't keep this commandment? Who helps us love others the way we want to be loved?

Older children and adults may read: Mark 12:28–34

Let's pray: Dear Jesus, You loved us more than You loved Yourself. Please help us learn from You how to love others. Forgive our selfish love. Give us the Holy Spirit so that we will love others the way we would like to be loved. Amen.

There are different kinds of working, but the same God works all of them in all [people]. 1 Corinthians 12:6

Many Ways of Serving Jesus

Kelsey and Tara were twins who lived in the lumber country of Oregon. While they were still in high school, they started a Sunday school all by themselves in the little town in which they lived.

"If one of us could be a nurse," Kelsey said, "she could earn enough money so the other one could work for Jesus every day. The children in these towns need to learn about God and His Word."

"That's a wonderful idea," agreed Tara. "I don't know which I'd rather be. A nurse can work for Jesus too."

The sisters decided to break a toothpick into two different-sized pieces. Whoever drew the shortest piece would try to become a nurse.

This may not have been the best way to decide, but the girls didn't care who won. They both just wanted to do something for Jesus. Kelsey drew the short piece, so she went to nurse's training.

While Kelsey studied to be a nurse, Tara got a job to help pay for her sister's training. She also kept teaching children at the Sunday school.

When Kelsey became a nurse, she gave half of her salary to her sister. Then Tara quit her job, bought a car, and started going to 14 different towns every week. Each day she visited homes, told Bible stories to children, and helped people learn about Jesus and His love.

The Bible says, "There are different kinds of working, but the same God works all of them in all [people]." The Holy Spirit leads us to love Jesus and His word, and then helps us find ways to work for God in whatever we do.

⟿

Let's talk: How did Kelsey and Tara work for God while they were still in high school? What did they do after they finished high school? How did one help the other do God's work? Which one do you think served God best? What does the Bible verse say? What are some other ways people work for Jesus? What can we do for Him?

Older children and adults may read: 1 Corinthians 12:4–11

Let's pray: O Holy Spirit, make us willing to live for Jesus, who died for us. Since there are many ways to work for Him, please help us find the best way for us. Amen.

I have hidden Your Word in my heart that I might not sin against You. Psalm 119:11

How Maeko Learned a Bible Verse

"I can't learn this Bible verse," said Maeko.

"What verse is it?" her mother asked.

"This one," said Maeko, and she read, "I have hidden Your Word in my heart that I might not sin against You."

"Let's see if I can make it easier for you," said Mother. "This verse tells of a good thing in a good place for a good reason. What's the good thing and the good place and the good reason?"

Maeko read the verse again. "God's Word—is that the good thing?" she asked.

"Yes, go on," said Mother.

"I have hidden Your Word in my heart," she read. "That must be the good place—my heart."

"And what's the good reason for hiding the good thing in the good place?" Mother asked.

" 'That I might not sin against You.' That's a good reason," answered Maeko.

Now Maeko knew the three parts: the good thing, in a good place, for a good reason. With that help, she easily said the verse from memory. What's more, she also learned what the verse meant. God's Word kept in our hearts keeps us from sinning. Memorizing God's Word puts it deep down in our hearts and helps us avoid sin.

Let's talk: What did Maeko have a hard time learning? How did Mother help her learn her memory verse? What's the good thing to hide? What's the good place to hide it? What's the good reason for hiding the good thing in the good place? Memorize the Bible verse.

Older children and adults may read: Psalm 119:9–16

Let's pray: Dear Lord, please help us hide Your Word in our hearts. Help us remember Your love and know Your will. And give us the Holy Spirit so that we will gladly obey You out of love for Jesus, our Savior. In His name we pray. Amen.

Jesus said, "If you hold to My teaching, ... you will know the truth." John 8:31–32

When a Man's Watch Stopped

"I have plenty of time to catch my train," said Mr. Burr. So he sat down and read the paper. A little later he looked at his watch again. It was still the same time as before.

"Oh, no!" he cried. "My watch stopped."

Mr. Burr rushed to the station, but before he got there, the train pulled out.

Some people miss life with God and heaven because they stop studying His Word and believing in Him. And that's a lot worse than missing a train. How do we know the truth about God? Jesus said, "If you hold to My teaching, ... you will know the truth."

We have family devotions because we want to live with Jesus. We study the Bible to keep believing what He has said. We go to church to hear and learn His Word so that we will know more about the truth. In all these activities, Jesus sends the Holy Spirit to strengthen our faith and pull us even closer to God.

It's important to continue believing the Bible. The Bible is the Word of God. It's the truth about how we are saved. What does the Bible say about God and the way to heaven? It says, "Believe in the Lord Jesus, and you will be saved." It says that through faith in Jesus, we get to live forever in heaven. It says, "Christ died for all."

We will not miss the train to heaven. Jesus keeps us ready to go.

Let's talk: Why did Mr. Burr miss his train? How can we know what is true about God and life with God? What did Jesus say we must hold to so that we can know the truth? How do we hold on to God's Word? Memorize the Bible verse.

Older children and adults may read: 2 Timothy 3:14–17

Let's pray: Dear Jesus, please help us keep believing Your Word. Bless our reading of the Bible, our family devotions, our church and Sunday schools, and anything else that helps us learn about the truth of life with God. Please keep us from believing any teachings that aren't true. Take us to be with You forever in heaven through Your love. In Your name we pray. Amen.

Let us not become weary in doing good. Galatians 6:9

Never Too Tired to Do Good

The telephone rang in the middle of a cold, rainy night. Pastor Hill answered, half asleep. The voice on the telephone said, "My wife is very sick. The ambulance is taking her to the hospital. I think she's going to die. Please come see her right away."

Pastor Hill dressed quickly, grabbed his coat and hat, and hurried to the hospital.

By then his daughter, Susan, was sitting up in bed.

"Mommy," said Susan, "people always call Daddy at night. He needs to sleep. Doesn't he ever get tired of helping people?"

"Your daddy has learned a Bible verse that helps him when he needs to leave at night. Would you like to learn it?" Mommy asked.

Susan nodded yes, so Mommy sat down beside her and told her, "Let us not become weary in doing good."

"Daddy never gets tired of doing good?" asked Susan.

"Oh, sometimes he does," said Mommy. "But Daddy's glad he can help others. He loves Jesus, and someday Jesus will say to him, 'What you did for others, you did for Me.' "

"I know," said Susan. "Even if you give just a drink of water to someone because you love Jesus, it's the same as giving it to Jesus. May I have a drink, Mommy?"

"Sure, but then we'd better go to sleep," said Mommy

with a smile. "Otherwise we might be too tired to do good tomorrow."

⤳

Let's talk: Why did Pastor Hill's phone ring in the middle of the night? Why did he get dressed and leave? What Bible verse did Susan's mother teach her? What did Jesus say about the good things people do for others?

Older children and adults may read: Matthew 25:31–40

Let's pray: Lord God, we're glad that You never get tired of being good to us. Please forgive us when we get tired of helping others. Keep us from ever getting tired of doing good. In Jesus' name we ask this. Amen.

All of you who were baptized into Christ have clothed yourselves with Christ. Galatians 3:27

When Anthony Was Adopted

Anthony's parents adopted him. After he had lived with his new father and mother for a year, they signed some papers. The papers said Anthony was really and truly their son. Now nobody could ever say he didn't belong to them.

Anthony's new parents loved him as their own son long before they signed the adoption papers. But they loved him even more after he belonged to them for keeps.

Baptism is like adoption. The Bible says, "All of you who were baptized into Christ have clothed yourselves with Christ." Through Baptism, people receive the faith in Jesus that makes them children of God.

Long ago fathers gave special coats to their children to show who belonged to them. When we were baptized, we put on the coat of Jesus Christ. This means we receive His name and life. Baptism is God's way of signing our adoption papers. That's why Baptism is sometimes called our second birthday, the day when we were adopted into God's family as a brother or sister of Jesus.

And do you know the most wonderful thing about being adopted by God? His children are given a home with Him in heaven! That's why our Baptism is so important. It reminds us that we have been adopted by God and that we belong to Him.

⌒

Let's talk: How did Anthony get new parents? Why were the papers they signed so important? What happens when people are baptized? What's so wonderful about being adopted by God?

Older children and adults may read: Galatians 3:26–29

Let's pray: Dear Father in heaven, we thank You for adopting us into Your family of people who believe in Jesus. Please wash away all our sins every day and keep us forever as Your children, through Jesus Christ, our Lord. Amen.

A happy heart makes the face cheerful. Proverbs 15:13

How to Be Cheerful

"Nothing ever goes right for me," said Marina. "I wanted to be invited to Kendall's party and I wasn't. I wanted to go swimming this afternoon, and now it's raining. I wanted to watch the murder movie on television, and Mom wouldn't let me. Everything's always wrong for me."

So Marina whined and complained. It wasn't good for

her either. She made herself sick and unhappy. She walked around with a sad face. She made other people feel sad too.

The Bible says, "A happy heart makes the face cheerful. Because Marina was sad, her face was sad, and she didn't have much spirit for anything.

How could Marina live without a sad face and a sick spirit? Well, she could start by saying, "I have lots of reasons for being happy. Jesus loves me, and God is good to me. I have a nice home and good parents. I'll do something for Mom or invite a friend to come over. Being happy is more important than seeing a movie or going to a party."

Marina could have enjoyed helping someone—perhaps someone in her family or a friend. She could have tried to make someone else happy. Then she would have felt better and she would have looked better.

When we believe in Jesus, Jesus lives in us and gives us the Holy Spirit. The Holy Spirit gives us a happy heart and a cheerful face because with Jesus we know that everything turns out for the best. That's another reason we like having Jesus in our hearts. Jesus keeps us happy, no matter what happens.

Let's talk: Why was Marina sad? How did her sad heart make her look? How do you think she acted? What does the Bible verse say? How does Jesus give us a happy heart? What kind of face does Jesus want us to have?

Older children and adults may read: Psalm 100

Let's pray: Dear God, help us to remember how much You love us so we won't whine and complain when we don't get what we want. Send Your Holy Spirit to make us happy and cheerful, through Jesus Christ, our Savior. Amen.

Turn away from evil. Proverbs 3:7 (RSV)

A Good Rule for Your Club

Six boys were starting a club. They were talking about rules.

"Let's have a rule that every member must skip school once a month," said Chad. "That'll keep out the sissies."

"Yeah, and let's make every member try to steal a candy bar from the grocery store. That'll be fun," said Toshiro.

"Well, I guess I can't join your club," said Enrique. "If you don't want to do things God's way, I don't want to belong."

"Aw, these rules are just to show we're not sissies," said Toshiro.

"I'd rather follow the Bible rule that says, 'Turn away from evil.' I think you should too," Enrique told them. "You're all Christians, aren't you?"

"Sure, but where'd you find that rule?" asked Chad.

"In the Bible. I'll show you the next time, if you want to see it," said Enrique. "It could be the first rule of our club, and then we'd have something we wouldn't have to be ashamed of."

Damone hadn't said anything yet. He'd been worrying about doing something wrong. But now he jumped up. "That's great!" he said. "I'd like that for our first rule."

So everyone agreed that the first rule of the club would be, "Turn away from evil."

That's a good rule for any club. You see, Jesus came and died to save us from sin and evil. He wants us to belong to His club—God's family. When we're members of *His* club, Jesus helps us turn away from evil. And He forgives us when we do sin. God's family is the best club to belong to.

Let's talk: Which rules did Chad and Toshiro want for their club? What did Enrique say about this? Which rule did Enrique want? Why was this a better rule? Whose club does Jesus want us to join? Who can be members? How does He make us members?

Older children and adults may read: Proverbs 1:10–15

Let's pray: We thank You, dear Father in heaven, for friends who help us turn away from evil. Please give us many such friends and make us glad to do things Your way. We ask this in the name of Jesus, who saved us from all evil. Amen.

You are the God who sees me. Genesis 16:13

When God Sees Us

"I don't like God," said Kiki. She was only 4 years old and didn't understand God very well.

"Why don't you like God, honey?" her mother asked.

" 'Cause God always watches me when I do bad," said Kiki.

"Don't you like me and Daddy?" Mother asked.

"Sure," said Kiki.

"Well, we watch you when you're bad," Mother told her.

"But you help me when I'm bad," Kiki explained.

"Honey, God does too," Mother said. "Yesterday you ran across the street, even though you shouldn't. God saw you and kept the cars from hitting you. He was good to you. But I think He's waiting for you to tell Him you're sorry."

"When I'm sorry, does God forgive me?" Kiki asked.

"Yes," said Mother, "He forgives you because He loves you. And do you remember why He forgives you?"

" 'Cause Jesus paid for my badness," said Kiki.

The Bible tells us that God sees all that we do. But when God watches us, He does it with love. And when we sin, He teaches us that it's wrong and moves us to ask Him for forgiveness. For Jesus' sake, God forgives us.

Let's talk: Why didn't Kiki like God? Why don't we want anyone to see what we do wrong? Why is it good that God always sees what we do? When we do wrong, what does God do? Why does God forgive us?

Older children and adults may read: Genesis 16:6–14

Let's pray: Dear Father in heaven, we're glad that You

never sleep and that You are always watching over us. Please watch that nothing bad happens to us. When we do wrong, please forgive us and help us to change. When we do right, help us to feel happy about it. In Jesus' name we ask it. Amen.

He who goes about as a talebearer reveals secrets, but he who is trustworthy in spirit keeps a thing hidden.
Proverbs 11:13 (RSV)

Is Tattling Wrong?

As the Meyers family ate supper, Isaac thought about what had happened at school that day.

"Darissa always tells the teacher everything we do," said Isaac. "It's wrong to be a tattletale, isn't it, Dad?"

"That depends on what a person tells," said Dad. "Maybe Darissa wants the teacher to help everyone behave better."

"No, she just likes to tattle," said Isaac. "And it's never about anything that's very important."

"Darissa can be pretty mean," agreed Isaac's sister, Cassie. "She's a real gossip. She's always talking about other people."

"Well, aren't you two talking about somebody at our supper table?" Mother asked.

Cassie looked at Isaac, and they both giggled. They realized they had been tattling on Darissa.

Sometimes things should be told. When we can help someone avoid doing wrong or keep a person from being hurt, we ought to tell what we know. But most tattling is wrong because it's gossip. Gossip hurts people and helps nobody.

The Bible says a talebearer (or tattletale) reveals secrets, but a person who has a trustworthy spirit keeps things hidden. This is true of secrets people tell us. It's also true of bad things we find out about people.

Jesus died for our sins. He has saved us from a tattling tongue. Because we love Jesus and others, we don't tell things that should be kept a secret.

Let's talk: When is it right to tell a secret we know? When is it wrong? Why was Darissa's tattling wrong? What does the Bible verse say about a talebearer or tattletale? What kind of person tries to keep a secret? How does loving Jesus keep us from having a tattling tongue?

Older children and adults may read: Proverbs 11:9–13

Let's pray: Father in heaven, please keep us from talking about other people. Help us to say only what's helpful. Make us willing to keep bad things a secret unless we can help someone. We ask this in Jesus' name. Amen.

She did what she could. Mark 14:8

A Little Light That Saved a Life

A long time ago, a young boy was sailing across the ocean. One night, just before he went to bed, he heard someone shouting, "Man overboard!" Then he heard many people running on the deck above him.

"What can I do?" he asked himself. "Up there I'll only be in the way."

Then he had an idea. He took the light that was hanging from the ceiling of his cabin and held it out of the porthole. He did this so that the light would shine on the water.

Soon he heard a voice yell, "We have him," and then some people in the crowd above shouted, "He's saved!"

The next day the captain told the passengers and crew that the light from the porthole helped save the man who fell overboard. The boy had done what he could, and it made the difference.

We usually are most helpful when we do what we can where we are. And Christians have a special reason for doing what they can. They have the love of Jesus in their hearts.

Once a woman named Mary wanted to do something that showed she loved Jesus. She poured some very expensive perfume on His head and feet. When guests at the dinner party scolded her for doing this, Jesus said, "Leave her alone. ... She has done a beautiful thing. ... She did what she could."

In another place, the Bible says, "Whatever your hand finds to do, do it with all your might." God wants us to do whatever we can as well as we can. The love of Jesus makes us want to do our very best for Him. Nothing but our best is good enough when we are giving Jesus our life. And we can ask the Holy Spirit make everything we do a pleasing gift to God.

Let's talk: What happened on the ship? What did the boy do to help? Why was this the best he could do? What special reason do we have for doing what we can to help people?

Older children and adults may read: Romans 16:1–6

Let's pray: Dear Lord, please lead us to do whatever we can for You and for others. Help us do it with all our might for the sake of Jesus, our Savior, who did so much for us. Amen.

Who can say, "I have kept my heart pure"? Proverbs 20:9

Our Clean Isn't Clean

"Simeon, did you wash? Are your hands and face clean?" his mother asked when he came to the table.

"Sure," he said. "I'm clean. I washed really good."

But when Simeon's mother looked at him closely, she saw that his ears were dirty, his face wasn't washed, and his hands had dirt between the fingers.

"Do you call that clean?" Mother asked Simeon as she showed him his hands.

"They look clean to me," he said.

"Your clean isn't very clean," Mother told him and made Simeon go back and wash again.

When God tells people their hearts must be clean for them to live in heaven, they say, "We're clean. We washed ourselves. We did some good things." But when God looks at them, He sees that their clean isn't His clean.

In our Bible verse, God asks, "Who can say, 'I have kept my heart pure'?" The answer is "Nobody." Nobody can make himself clean from sin. We all need to ask God to wash away the dirt of sin.

When Simeon's mother washed him, he was clean. When God washes away all our sins by forgiving us for Jesus' sake, then we are clean from head to toe—we're really clean.

Let's talk: Who thought Simeon was clean? Who didn't think so? How did Simeon become clean? What does God say to us when we think we've made ourselves clean? What's the only way we get clean from sin?

Older children and adults may read: Romans 4:5–8

Let's pray: Dear Father in heaven, don't let us ever think we're clean when we really aren't. We want to be with You in heaven, and we know that we can't make ourselves clean enough for that. So please wash our hearts by forgiving all our sins for Jesus' sake. In His name we ask this. Amen.

We have been made holy. Hebrews 10:10

A Holy Man in a Hardware Store

"Here comes a holy man," Mr. James whispered to his wife as they stood in the hardware store's checkout lane. He didn't want Mr. Crane to hear him, but Mr. Crane did.

"That's true," said Mr. Crane. "A holy man is standing behind you."

Mr. and Mrs. James laughed. "Go ahead and laugh," said Mr. Crane, "but the Bible says I'm a holy man."

"Look, last time we met, you tried to tell me all people are sinners," Mr. James said. "When I told you that most people are good, you said, 'Not good enough for God.' Remember? And now you say you're holy?"

"But I am," responded Mr. Crane. "You see, I do many wrong things, so I'm a sinner. But God forgives me for Jesus' sake. The Bible says, 'The blood of Jesus, God's Son, cleanses us from all sin.' That means I'm also clean and holy. In God's eyes, I'm a saint as well as a sinner because He takes away my sins."

"I thought only saints were holy," said Mrs. James.

"You're right. But I'm a saint, even though it may not sound right for me to say it," said Mr. Crane. "You can be too. The Bible calls all the followers of Jesus 'saints.' God doesn't call people saints because they're perfect in what

they do. They're called saints because they believe in Jesus and have their sins washed away."

That night Mr. and Mrs. James talked for a long time about Mr. Crane and what he had said. "So that's why Christians say, 'I believe in the communion of saints,' " said Mrs. James. "I think we need the love of Jesus too."

$$\approx$$

Let's talk: What did Mr. James call Mr. Crane? Why did Mr. and Mrs. James laugh when Mr. Crane said he was holy? How does God make us holy? Why does the Bible call Christians "saints"? Do you think you are a holy saint? Do you always act like a saint? Why not? Who helps us act like saints?

Older children and adults may read: 2 Timothy 1:8–12

Let's pray: Dear Father in heaven, we're glad that through Your forgiveness we are holy, even though we are sinners. Please forgive our sins every day for Jesus' sake, and help us live a holy life for You. In Jesus' name we ask this. Amen.

We have an advocate. 1 John 2:1

A Helper to Get Us Through

Isabel, Anton, and their mother were flying to America. Their father was dead, and they were very poor. They had been living in a camp for refugees. Someone in America had promised to take care of them.

"What do we have to do when we land?" Anton asked Mr. Adler, the man traveling with them. "We can't talk English very well, we don't have any money, and we don't know how to act in America."

Mr. Adler smiled. "Don't worry. I'll help you. That's why I'm here," he said. "I'll get you to where you're going. And at the other end, you have a lawyer who will take care of you."

Anton turned to his mother. "Mr. Adler said he'll help us, and we have a lawyer in America who will take care of us," he told his mother and sister. Then they all felt much better. They could hardly wait to get to their new home.

Some Christians worry about what will happen to them when they die. They have many sins. They know they can't pay for their sins themselves. They wonder whether they will get to their home in heaven or whether God might refuse to let them in.

The Bible says we have an advocate. An advocate is someone who speaks for us, like lawyers speak for their clients. Our lawyer and helper is Jesus Christ. He is with God the Father in heaven and has arranged a place for us in heaven. He has even paid the cost of our home in heaven by living and dying and rising again for us. He has promised to be with us all the way to heaven.

While we're here on earth, Jesus has given us many people to help us on the way to heaven. Can you name some of them?

Let's talk: Why was Anton worried? What made him feel better? Why do we need a lawyer? Who has promised to get us to heaven?

Older children and adults may read: 1 John 1:7–2:2

Let's pray: Lord Jesus, we're glad that You are our lawyer in heaven. Please wash away all our sins, and keep us on the path to our heavenly home. Thank You also for the people who help us on our way. Amen.

One who is slack in his work is brother to one who destroys.
Proverbs 18:9

There's No Fun Like Work

"How much work do you have to do at home?" Elise asked Noelle.

"I'm supposed to clear the table before going to school and make my bed and set the supper table and take care of my dog," said Noelle. "But I know how to get out of work."

"How?" asked Elise.

"I waste a lot of time getting ready, and when there's no time left, Mom says, 'Hurry up, get out of here, or you'll be late for school!' Then I don't have to do anything," answered Noelle.

"But you'll never learn to work that way," said Elise. "My dad says, 'There's no fun like work.' "

"You think work is fun?" asked Noelle. "I get out of it when I can."

"But what'll you do when you *have* to work?" Elise asked. "You won't enjoy working. Remember what our teacher said? People who amount to something usually like to work. And God wants us to be useful."

Elise was right. The Bible calls the lazy person wicked. It says, "One who is slack in his work is brother to one who destroys." That means a lazy person is an bad as one who wastes a lot. Lazy people waste their time.

God wants us to be useful and busy for Him. We can't be if we're lazy. That's why laziness is a sin for which we

need the forgiveness of Jesus, our Savior. We can ask Jesus for forgiveness and to help us do our work happily. And He will forgive us and help us. It's really a lot of fun to work hard for God.

Let's talk: How did Noelle feel about work? What did Elise tell her? What does the Bible call a lazy person? What does the lazy person waste? Who forgives us and helps us work happily? Memorize the Bible verse.

Older children and adults may read: Proverbs 24:30–34

Let's pray: Lord Jesus, when You were a boy, You were helpful to others. When You were a young man, You worked hard as a carpenter. When You were a preacher and teacher, You hardly had time to eat and sleep. Please make us willing to work hard for You. Amen.

The Lord hates ... a false witness who pours out lies.
Proverbs 6:19

The Sin of Whispering Lies

Mrs. Burns often went to Mrs. Scott's house. They liked to have a cup of coffee together and sit and talk.

"You know," said Mrs. Burns, "Mrs. Rielly treats her husband really bad. And she's a messy housekeeper."

"I know," agreed Mrs. Scott. "Why one time I saw her putting dishes away that were only half clean."

They talked about many people that way. Mrs. Burns and Mrs. Scott seemed to always tell bad things about others, most of them lies.

Mrs. Rielly didn't know why some of her friends were avoiding her. She didn't know that Mrs. Burns and Mrs. Scott were telling lies about her.

One day Mrs. Burns went over to Mrs. Lander's house. "You know, I must tell you, Mrs. Rielly across the street is having a lot of trouble with her husband," Mrs. Burns whispered.

"Oh, I think they get along better than most of our neighbors," responded Mrs. Lander.

"But she's a messy housekeeper," added Mrs. Burns.

"You must be wrong," said Mrs. Lander. "She helped clean here for me when I was sick. She's the cleanest, neatest person you've ever met."

"Well, good-bye, it was nice visiting with you," huffed Mrs. Burns. She was angry. She didn't like people who wouldn't listen to her lies.

There are many people like Mrs. Burns. In fact, sometimes we all like to repeat bad stories about people. Sometimes we enjoy whispering lies that get other people in trouble.

But telling lies in a whisper or out loud is a sin. The Bible says, "The Lord hates ... a false witness who pours out lies." That's why He has given us the commandment, "You shall not give false witness against your neighbor."

The lies we tell are why Jesus had to suffer and die for us. God would have to punish us if Jesus hadn't paid for our sins. Because Jesus took our punishment, we show our love for Him by trying not to tell lies.

Let's talk: What did Mrs. Burns and Mrs. Scott like to say? How did Mrs. Lander make Mrs. Burns angry? How does the Lord feel about a false witness? Which commandment tells us not to lie? Why do Christians try not to lie?

Older children and adults may read: Proverbs 6:12–19

Let's pray: Lord Jesus, You never told lies or repeated bad stories about anyone. Thank You for taking our punishment for the lies we tell. Teach us to say only what is good and helpful. Amen.

Your Father in heaven is not willing that any of these little ones should be lost. Matthew 18:14

Some Very Foolish Sheep

Cal was helping his father bring home their sheep. There were wolves in the woods nearby, so Cal and his father put the sheep into a pen at night to keep them safe.

When Cal opened the little gate in the fence, some of the sheep didn't want to go into the pen. They ran past the gate.

"Let's let them stay out," said Cal. "I'm getting tired. It'll be their own fault if the wolves get them."

"No, I don't want any of my sheep to be killed by a wolf," answered Dad, so they kept trying to get the sheep through the gate.

Jesus once said, "I am the gate for the sheep." Jesus is the gate through which we have to go to be saved and safe. The devil and his angels are the wolves. They want to grab us and keep us from getting to heaven.

Many people don't know this. They don't want to go through the little gate. They refuse to believe that Jesus is their Savior.

But Jesus loves us. He said, "Your Father in heaven doesn't want a single little lamb to die." Jesus, the Good Shepherd, died for His Father's sheep—for us. And we want others to be in the sheep pen with us, so we tell our family and friends about our Good Shepherd, Jesus.

Let's talk: Why did Cal and his father try to put their sheep into a safe place? Why was it hard? Why didn't they give up? What did Jesus do to save us? Why is Jesus the "gate" of God's sheep pen? What did Jesus say His Father doesn't want? How can we help others become Jesus' sheep?

Older children and adults may read: Psalm 23

Let's pray: Dear Father in heaven, thank You for saving us from the devil by bringing us into Your kingdom through Jesus, the gate. Help us tell others about our Good Shepherd, so they will become His sheep too. In Jesus' name we pray. Amen.

Endure hardship with us like a good soldier of Christ Jesus.
2 Timothy 2:3

Following Jesus the Hard Way

"I want to be a doctor," said Skye. "But I don't want to go to college a long time."

"That's the only way to become a doctor," said her brother Logan.

"Then I'll be a lawyer," said Skye.

"You'll have to study law then," said Logan. "That takes a long time too."

"Well, then I'll be a teacher," said Skye.

"Don't you think teachers have to go to school many years?" asked Logan.

"How about a pastor? At least you won't have to go to school a long time to be a pastor," said Skye.

"Yes, I will—as much as a doctor, and sometimes more," said Logan, grinning. He wanted to be a pastor. "There should be an easy way to become a doctor or a lawyer or a teacher or a pastor," Skye grumbled.

"There just isn't," said Logan. "You won't amount to much by just doing the things that are easy. Sometimes you've got to go the hard way."

"But it's easy to be a Christian," said Skye. "All you have to do is believe in Jesus."

"Maybe it's easy to *become* a Christian, but to *be* a Christian takes a lot of studying and praying," said Logan. "That's why Paul told Timothy, 'Endure hardship with us like a good soldier of Christ Jesus.' That means, do the hard things for Jesus like He did."

Skye thought about this awhile. "Maybe I'll become a missionary doctor, even if I have to study a long time," she said. "A missionary doctor could help Jesus a lot."

Let's talk: Why didn't Skye want to become a doctor or a teacher? What did Logan tell her about doing only easy things? What did Paul tell Timothy about being a soldier of Jesus? What do you think he meant? Why is it easy to *become* a Christian? Why is it hard to *be* a Christian? Why are Christians willing to do hard things for Jesus?

Older children and adults may read: 2 Corinthians 11:23–28

Let's pray: Dear Jesus, You didn't follow an easy road when You lived and died to save us and to give us life with God in heaven. Please make us willing to do hard things for You, especially those things that will be helpful to others. Amen.

They were longing for a better country—a heavenly one.
Therefore God is not ashamed to be called their God.
Hebrews 11:16

God and All Kinds of People

"Mother, I'm supposed to march in the school parade with Elizabeth," complained Jill, making a face that plainly said she didn't want to do it.

"What's so bad about that?" Mother asked.

"Elizabeth doesn't have nice clothes," Jill explained. "Her parents are poor."

"Is that a reason to be ashamed of her?" asked Mother.

"But Elizabeth isn't like the rest of us," grumbled Jill. "I'll feel silly walking with her."

"Elizabeth goes to the same church we do. She loves the Lord Jesus and will be in heaven with us," Mother said. "I'm sure God isn't ashamed of her."

"How do you know?" asked Jill stubbornly.

Mother got her Bible. The verse she was looking for was highlighted in neon yellow.

"Look here, in the book of Hebrews. It tells about all kinds of people who loved God because they believed His promise of a home with Him in heaven," Mother said. "Hebrews 11:16 says, 'God is not ashamed to be called their God.' God is not ashamed to be called the God of anybody who wants to live with Him and believes His promises. God isn't ashamed to be Elizabeth's God."

"But do I have to be friends with everybody?" Jill argued.

Mother was sad that Jill didn't want to be friendly with all children.

"Some people are proud. They think they're too good to be with people who are poor or from a different country," she said. "Others aren't kind to people whose skin is a different color than theirs. But the Bible says, 'Anyone who loves God and believes what is right is accepted by God.' If God isn't ashamed to be their God, how can we be ashamed to be their friends?"

Jill didn't say anything more. But she was friendly with Elizabeth when they marched together in the parade. Later she told her mother, "I'm glad God loves all people, especially those who want to be with Him in heaven."

Let's talk: What was Jill worried about? What did Mother tell her? What does God say about anyone who loves Him? Why are some people ashamed to be friendly with others? Why was Jill willing to be friendly with Elizabeth?

Older children and adults may read: Hebrews 11:13–16

Let's pray: Lord God, our Father in heaven, we're glad that You aren't ashamed of those who love You. Thanks especially for not being ashamed of us. Please help us not to be ashamed of being friendly to other people, especially to people who are Your children. We ask this in the name of Jesus, who died for all. Amen.

Christ suffered for you, leaving you an example, that you should follow in His steps. 1 Peter 2:21

Following the Pattern

"What's the matter with this stupid cloth, Mom?" complained Corinne. She was almost crying. She was learning to sew, but the dress she was making didn't fit or look right.

Mother looked at the dress. "Nothing's wrong with the

cloth, honey," she said. "You just didn't follow the pattern."

If Corinne had followed the pattern carefully, her dress would have turned out all right. A good pattern shows you how to make something.

And Corinne isn't the only one who doesn't follow the pattern. Even adults forget.

"What's the matter with our home?" asked Mr. Blake. "There's so much arguing and unhappiness."

Do you know what's causing the trouble? He and his family probably aren't following God's pattern for life in their home.

"I don't know what's wrong with my life," said Miss Gregson. "I don't know why I'm even alive."

There's an easy answer for Miss Gregson. If Jesus were a part of her life, He would give her an easy pattern to follow that would make her life worthwhile.

"Our church is a mess," said Mrs. Moss. "We argue in every meeting, and no one wants to do any work."

Mrs. Moss' church should ask Jesus to help them follow His pattern for their work. Then they will be His happy, willing workers.

The Bible says, "Christ suffered for you, leaving you an example, that you should follow in His steps." Jesus is the pattern. When we follow Him, our church and our home and our life become what God wants them to be.

Let's talk: Why didn't the dress Corinne was making turn out right? What pattern has God given us to follow in our lives? What has Jesus done that we should follow? What did Jesus do that gives us reason to follow Him? What are some ways we can follow Him?

Older children and adults may read: 1 Peter 2:20–25

Let's pray: Lord Jesus, we can't love as You loved, nor live as good a life as You lived. Please forgive us. For Your sake, help us follow Your pattern so that we will be more like You in all that we do. Amen.

[God] is able to do immeasurably more than all we ask or imagine. Ephesians 3:20

They Got More than They Asked For

"I wish Mr. Glass would tell us we could pick some of his cherries. His trees are loaded," said Allison.

"Why don't we ask him?" asked Toby, her brother.

"He'll just say no and try to scare us away," explained Allison.

But Toby still thought it wouldn't hurt to ask. The next afternoon, Toby saw Mr. Glass in his orchard. He walked over and asked, "Mr. Glass, do you ever let kids pick cherries?"

"I might," answered Mr. Glass. "But you'd have to pick around the bottom and stay out of the trees. I don't want you to get hurt, you know."

"Great!" said Toby. "Thanks."

"And when the plums and apples get ripe, you can pick some of them too." said Mr. Glass. "God gives me much more than I can use by myself."

Toby ran to tell Allison the good news. "We got even more than I asked for," he said.

In a way, God is a lot like Mr. Glass. God is glad when we ask Him for things that are good for us, and He gives us much more than we ask. The Bible says, "God can do immeasurably more than all that we ask or imagine." He even gives us everlasting life with Him. He does this for the sake of Jesus Christ, our Lord and Savior.

Let's talk: What did Toby and Allison wish? Why didn't Allison want to ask Mr. Glass? What did Mr. Glass say when Toby talked to him? How is God like Mr. Glass? What is the best gift God gives us? How do we get this gift?

Older children and adults may read: Ephesians 3:14–21

Let's pray: Dear Father in heaven, help us trust that You love us and will give us much more than all we could ever

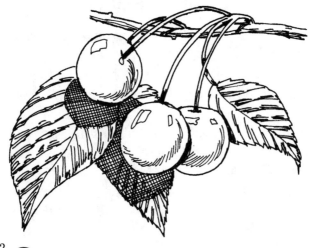

ask for or imagine. We're glad that we're Your children through Jesus Christ, our Savior. In His name we pray. Amen.

The church in their house. Romans 16:5 (RSV)

The Family Altar

The first time Neesha attended her new Sunday school at Trinity Church, the teacher asked everyone to bring money for an altar.

"Why do you need money to have an altar?" asked Neesha.

"We would like to have our own little altar to gather around while we visit with God," explained Mrs. Graeler. "We can't have an altar unless we can pay someone to make it."

"In our home we have a family altar, but it's not a table," said Neesha.

Mrs. Graeler smiled. "Tell us about it," she invited.

So Neesha came forward. "The first thing my daddy wanted in our new house was family devotions. So when we moved in, we all sat in the living room, and he read from the Bible," Neesha explained. "Then we all knelt and asked God to bless us in our new home. Daddy said our devotions together every day would be our family altar."

"Thank you for telling us about your family altar," said Mrs. Graeler. "I wish everyone had a family altar in their home. When you read and listen to God's Word and pray with your family in your home, then you have family devotions. That's like having a church service in your house. And that kind of altar doesn't cost any money."

"Then why do we need money for a Sunday school altar?" asked Neesha.

"Because a special table where we meet with God helps us think about God," explained Mrs. Graeler. "That's why we want it to be beautiful. That's also why we put a cross and candles on the altar. They help us remember that Jesus our Savior died for us."

$\approx$

Let's talk: What did Mrs. Graeler ask Neesha's Sunday school to do? Why was Neesha puzzled? What kind of altar did Neesha have in her home? What is a family altar? How can an altar of wood help us? Which of the two altars is most important?

Older children and adults may read: Colossians 3:15–17

Let's pray: Dear God, we're glad that we can pray to You anywhere. Bless our family altar by speaking to us and listening to our prayers. Come into our hearts every day, through Jesus Christ, our Lord. In His name we pray. Amen.

God clothes the grass of the field. Matthew 6:30

What Flowers Tell about God

"The flowers are beautiful," Zoe said to Miss Welch, the lady from church. Miss Welch was visiting Zoe in the hospital, and she had brought flowers from the church. Visiting the sick was one of the ways Miss Welch worked for God.

"Flowers say many things to us," said Miss Welch. "They talk to us about God."

"They do?" asked Zoe.

"Yes, they do. They tell us that God loves us," explained

Miss Welch. "God could have made all the flowers one color. But why did He make flowers so colorful? Because He knew we would like pretty things."

"Now I can hear the flowers talk," said Zoe with a smile. "Here's one with three colors in one blossom, and it's so soft and lovely."

"Jesus said the flowers tell us not to worry," continued Miss Welch. "The flowers never worry about what to wear, but God gives them pretty clothes anyway. Jesus said the only thing we need to worry about is being a child of God and living with Him."

"I'm glad I'm God's child," said Zoe. "I believe that Jesus is God and that He died for me."

"Good, that means you have God's love, and your life can be as pretty as a flower," said Miss Welch. And she gave Zoe a big hug.

Let's talk: What did Miss Welch say to Zoe about flowers? What did Jesus say about flowers? What do flowers say to you? What made Zoe happy? Why did Miss Welch give Zoe a hug?

Older children and adults may read: Matthew 6:28–33

Let's pray: Dear God, we thank You for the flowers that tell us that You love us. We thank You most of all for the love of Jesus, who suffered and died so that we could be Your children. Please live in our hearts and make our lives as beautiful as flowers, through Jesus Christ, our Lord. In His name we pray. Amen.

The Lord knows those who are His. 2 Timothy 2:19

God Knows and We Don't

"Look, Mr. Rodriguez died yesterday," said Donnell's mother, pointing to an article in the newspaper. "He was the man who used to live on the corner."

"I remember," said Donnell. "Dad didn't think he was a good Christian because he wouldn't give any money for our new church."

"Yes, but do you remember what I said?" asked Mother. "Don't judge other people. Only God knows who the Christians are. This story in the paper shows that we were probably wrong about Mr. Rodriguez."

"What does it say?" asked Donnell.

"It says he had been paying all the expenses for a missionary in Peru," explained Mother.

"All the expenses? Then he was giving a lot to God! That must have been thousands of dollars a year!" Donnell gasped. "Probably more."

"You see?" said Mother. "We thought Mr. Rodriguez was stingy and didn't love God, but all the time he was giving more money for God's work than most people do."

"We can't ever know how much someone loves God, can we?" asked Donnell.

"No," answered Mother. "But we do know that Mr. Rodriguez was probably giving to that missionary because of what Jesus gave to him. Jesus gave His life for Mr. Rodriguez. Mr. Rodriguez' gift showed that Jesus lived in his heart. Mr. Rodriguez was a good Christian."

"Well, I guess that means we can't know for sure who the Christians are," Donnell decided.

"No, we can't ever know for sure," agreed Mother. "But God knows. The Bible says, 'The Lord knows those who are His,' and that's what counts."

Let's talk: What did Mother find out about Mr. Rodriguez when he died? Why was she surprised? What did she tell Donnell? Why can't we know for sure whether someone's a Christian? Who does know?

Older children and adults may read: Matthew 6:1–4

Let's pray: Heavenly Father, please forgive us for trying to judge others. We can't know what they believe or why they do things. Help us remember that You are the judge of all people and that You know who loves You and who doesn't.

Please fill our hearts with Your love so that we will show our love for You in many ways. We ask this through Jesus Christ, our Lord. Amen.

The sacrifices of God are a broken spirit. Psalm 51:17

Why the Sheep Were Burned

Kendrick and Paige were looking at pictures in a Bible storybook. When their father came and took a look too, Paige pointed to the picture of an altar. Smoke was going up from the altar. "What are they burning, Daddy?" she asked.

"They killed a sheep, and now they are having a church service," explained Dad. "After awhile, they'll eat most of the sheep. The part they are burning is called a sacrifice."

"What's a sacrifice, Dad?" asked Kendrick.

"It was a way of telling God, 'We're sorry that we've done wrong. Somebody must die to pay for our sins. Please let it be this sheep instead of us,' " Dad answered.

"Why did God want people to burn the sheep?" asked Kendrick.

"What God really cared about was how the people felt inside," Dad said. "If the people were sorry for their sins and wanted God to forgive them, then God was pleased."

"Like when we're sorry for our sins?" asked Paige.

"Yes," said Dad. "King David said, 'The sacrifices of God are a broken spirit.' A broken spirit is a willingness to say, 'I was wrong; I've sinned.' "

"I know a Bible verse that calls Jesus the Lamb of God," said Paige. "Look, the Lamb of God, who takes away the sin of the world!"

"Good girl," said Dad. "The sheep sacrifices were only reminders that God would send His Son, Jesus, to die for everybody's sins."

"Is that why we don't burn sheep in our church services?" asked Kendrick.

"That's right," said Dad. "Jesus came to be our sacrifice. Because He died, we don't have to make anymore sacrifices. Now when we sin and ask God for forgiveness, He remembers Jesus' sacrifice and forgives us."

Let's talk: What did the people in the Bible tell God with their sacrifices? Who was the Lamb of God who died for us? Why did God want the people in the Bible to burn sheep? What did King David say is the sacrifice that pleases God? What is a broken spirit? Why does God forgive us?

Older children and adults may read: Genesis 4:1–7

Let's pray: Dear Lord, our God, please take our prayer instead of a sheep as a way of telling You we are sorry for our sins. Forgive all our sins for Jesus' sake, who died for us. Give us the Holy Spirit to help us live lives that please You. In Jesus' name we pray. Amen.

Trust in the Lord. Psalm 37:3

On Board a Big Ship

Janice and her mother were crossing the ocean on a big ship. One evening as they walked hand in hand along the deck, Mother said, "You know, I've been thinking. This ship is like our life with God. Can you name some ways the two are alike?"

Janice thought awhile. "Well, we're traveling with many other people, and we don't know where we're going," said Janice. "And Jesus is our captain, and He'll take us where we need to go."

"Now wait a minute," said Mother. "You were mostly right, but don't you know where we're going?"

"Oh, sure," said Janice. "I meant we couldn't find the way by ourselves. We let the captain steer the ship."

"Very good," said Mother. "In church windows and in picture books, God's church is sometimes pictured as a ship. Who is the captain of that ship?"

"That's easy," said Janice. "Jesus is the captain of His Church."

Janice and her mother kept on walking and talking. "Could anyone get across the ocean without going on a ship?" Mother asked Janice.

"Well, they could fly or go on another boat," answered Janice. "But however they went, they'd need a captain who could take them to the right place."

"They couldn't get there by trying to swim across by themselves?" asked Mother.

"Of course not," said Janice, laughing.

"We can't get to heaven by ourselves," said Mother. "But Jesus, our Lord, knows the way. He takes all who are on His ship to their Father in heaven."

"And you know what?" asked Janice, "Jesus even paid our way."

"Yes," said Mother, giving Janice a little hug, "and He takes very good care of us on the way. That's why the Bible often tells us to trust in the Lord."

Let's talk: Where were Janice and her mother? What did they talk about? How is a ship or an airplane trip like life with God? Why can't we get to heaven by ourselves? What did Jesus pay so we could go to heaven? Why does the Bible tell us to trust in the Lord?

Older children and adults may read: Psalm 37:3–5

Let's pray: Dear Jesus, our captain on the way to heaven, we're glad that we're with You and that You are taking us to see our Father in heaven. Thank You for paying our way. Please keep us from ever leaving You and Your ship or from trying to get to heaven by ourselves. Help us always trust in You, for with You we're safe and in good care. Amen.

Be still before the LORD and wait patiently for Him; do not fret. Psalm 37:7

What Patience Means

Jaime had chicken pox, and his skin felt itchy. When there are scabs on the pox, children want to scratch them. And when they do, they can get little scars that never go away. They're called pockmarks.

The doctor knew she had to keep Jaime from scratching, so she told Jaime's parents to tie mittens on his hands. Jaime couldn't take off the mittens, and he could not get them off easily when he tried.

Jaime didn't like this at all. He complained and fretted. He wasn't a bit patient. He wanted to go out and play. And where the pocks were healing, Jaime wanted to scratch them so badly, he'd stomp his feet and cry and say mean things.

Soon the itching stopped, and the doctor said Jaime was better. The next day he went to see his friend Nico.

Nico also had chicken pox, but he was still sick. Nico was playing a game of dominoes by himself and seemed happy.

"How come they don't have to tie your mittens on you? How can you just sit there and be happy?" Jaime asked Nico.

"Oh, I'm waiting for God's time," explained Nico.

"God's time? What's God's time?" asked Jaime.

"Well, my mother told me the itching is God's time for healing the skin," answered Nico. "It would be wrong to complain and try to hurry God in what He has to do. I'm trying to wait patiently for the Lord to make me well. I play games or put together models or watch TV."

The Bible says, "Be still before the LORD and wait patiently for Him; do not fret." Trust that God loves you, and give God a chance to help you. He always helps His children, we just have to trust Him and wait patiently.

Let's talk: How did Jaime fret and complain? Why did he fret? Why did Nico act differently? What does the Bible say we should do instead of fretting? Why can we be sure that God will help us?

Older children and adults may read: Job 1:13–22

Let's pray: Sometimes, dear Lord, we don't understand what You are doing. We fret instead of waiting patiently for Your help. Please teach us to trust You more, knowing that You make things come out just right for those whom You love. In Jesus' name we pray. Amen.

There is not a righteous man on earth who does what is right and never sins. Ecclesiastes 7:20

A Good Man

Malik liked his new Sunday school superintendent a lot. "He's a really good guy!" Malik said at the supper table. Everybody agreed—except Adira.

"My teacher said nobody is completely good," Adira argued. "My teacher said everybody is a sinner."

"Oh, I know that," said Malik. "But we could still call him a good man the way people talk, couldn't we, Father?"

"Well, the Bible calls some people good and others wicked," Father pointed out. "But we don't ever want to get the idea that anyone is perfectly good. That wouldn't be true."

"But I still think Mr. Gordon is a good man, and I'm sure God thinks so too," said Malik.

"All right," said Adira, "but even a superintendent does some wrong things, and so do pastors and dads and moms and everybody."

"You're right, Adira," said Father. "Everybody does wrong things, including me, your Momma, and even Pastor Jefferson. That's why we all need God's forgiveness, and that's why we need to forgive each other all the time. The Bible says, 'There is not a righteous man on earth who does what is right and never sins.' "

"But I still think Mr. Gordon is a good man," Malik insisted.

"Sure he is," said Father. "But he's also a sinner. Mr. Gordon knows this and is very thankful for God's forgiveness. That's why he loves Jesus and does good things for Him."

⤸

Let's talk: What did Malik say about Mr. Gordon? Why did Adira say he wasn't good? Who was right? Why do we need to know that everybody sins? Who takes away our sins? How do we show Jesus we're thankful for our forgiveness?

Older children and adults may read: Job 1:1–5

Let's pray: O Lord, our God, we know that we're all sinners and that nobody but You is really good unless You make someone good. Please take away our sins for Jesus' sake, and give us the Holy Spirit so that we can obey Your commands. In Jesus' name we ask it. Amen.

[Jesus] is the atoning sacrifice for our sins, and not only for ours but also for the sins of the whole world. 1 John 2:2

Can God Forgive a Murderer?

In the paper one day there was a picture of a young man who had killed several people.

"God will punish him, won't He?" asked Rebecca. She sounded as though she hoped God would.

"That depends on whether the man asks for God's forgiveness," answered Mother.

"You mean he could kill someone and ask God to forgive him and then kill another person and be forgiven?" asked Rebecca.

"Yes, if he really was sorry both times, God would forgive him," responded Mother. "But if the man believed in Jesus and was *really* sorry the first time, he wouldn't kill again. When we ask God to forgive us and we *really* mean it, we don't want to do that sin again."

"But how can God forgive a person who murders other people?" asked Rebecca. She just couldn't believe it was possible.

"It's only because of what Jesus did for all of us," Mother explained. "The Bible says, 'Jesus paid for our sins, and not only for ours but also for the sins of the whole world.' That includes people who kill others."

"Then even the worst sinner in the whole world could get forgiveness from God," Rebecca pointed out.

Mother agreed. "Peter got forgiveness even though he cursed and said he didn't know Jesus," she said. "And Judas could have had forgiveness for selling Jesus if he had asked Jesus for it. Why don't we say a prayer for the murderer and ask God to change his heart?"

Rebecca and her mother prayed for the young man whose picture was in the paper. That night Rebecca's mother marked some verses in a booklet of the gospel of John. She wrote on the cover, "We prayed for you. Please read this." The next day she sent the booklet to the man in jail.

Let's talk: What did Rebecca think would happen to the murderer? What didn't Rebecca believe at first? Why does God forgive even a murderer? What did Rebecca and her mother do for the man in jail? Why did Mother send him the gospel of John? Memorize the Bible verse.

Older children and adults may read: James 5:16–20

Let's pray: Dear Father in heaven, please keep us from sinning. Help us remember that Jesus paid for all sins, even for the sin of murder. Forgive our sins, whatever they are, for Jesus' sake. Make us willing to tell others about Your great love in Christ Jesus, our Savior. In His name we pray. Amen.

In regard to evil be infants, but in your thinking be adults.
1 Corinthians 14:20

How Grown-Up Are You?

"Aw, he wouldn't know how," said Trevor, who was trying to get Luis to steal a toy gun from the discount store.

Luis was acting as though he didn't understand what Trevor and the other boys wanted him to do. Finally he said, "It isn't right to steal."

"Listen to the little Sunday school teacher talking," said Colton, who was trying to act big. "You gonna go tell your mom?"

Luis didn't let the boys pressure him into doing something wrong. "I don't care what you think," he said. "I'd rather be right with God."

The Bible says, "In regard to evil be infants, but in your thinking be adults." Luis didn't mind being called names for not wanting to steal. He was being a man in thinking the way God wanted him to think.

The devil gets people to think that doing what's wrong makes them more grown-up. But people who are grown-up in their thinking know how foolish it is to sin. It's much better to obey God.

Jesus, God's Son, was a real man. The Bible says He never sinned. Because we have Jesus in out hearts, He helps us become babies about badness but grown-up in our thinking.

~

Let's talk: Why did Trevor and Colton make fun of Luis? Why wasn't Luis ashamed to be called a Sunday school teacher? In what way should we be babies? What is grown-up thinking? Who helps us become grown-up in Christian thinking? Memorize the Bible verse.

Older children and adults may read: 1 Peter 4:1–5

Let's pray: Dear Lord, our God, please keep us from growing up in badness. Help us to be grown-up Christians so that we will understand and gladly follow Your ways, through Jesus Christ, our Savior. Amen.

*I trust in You, O L*ORD*; I say, "You are my God."* Psalm 31:14

Putting on Our Life Belt

There was a big hole in the front of the boat. It had run into another boat. When the captain saw that his boat was going to sink, he shouted, "Everybody get a life belt!"

The life belts the boat had were round with a hole in the middle. They went around the passengers' chests. They kept the people from sinking.

A boy stood on the deck holding his life belt and shivering with fear. "Put it on!" shouted the captain. "It won't do you a bit of good if you don't get into it."

"I don't think it can help me," said the boy. "Maybe it'll pull me under the water." He didn't trust the belt, so he didn't want to use the thing that could save his life.

The captain ran over, grabbed the belt out of the boy's hands, and pushed it over his head and arms. "There, now you'll float when you jump in the water," he said.

The Bible says, "Believe in the Lord Jesus, and you will be saved." Some people don't understand how believing in Jesus can save them. They don't trust Jesus. They don't believe He's their Savior. And because they don't believe, they will go to hell when they die, which is much worse than drowning.

"Clothe yourselves with the Lord Jesus Christ," the apostle Paul told the Romans. Jesus is like a life belt. Because we believe in Him, He saves us from our sins and their punishment. With the psalm writer we say, "I trust in You, O Lord; I say, 'You are my God.' "

⤳

Let's talk: What did the captain tell everyone on his boat to do? Why didn't the boy do it? How did the captain help save the boy? How is Jesus like a life belt? How are some people like the boy who didn't put on the life belt? Why do we trust God to save us? Whom do you know who needs to hear about Jesus?

Older children and adults may read: Psalm 32:5–11

Let's pray: We are trusting You, Lord Jesus, to take care of us here on earth and to take us to be with You in heaven. Make us more willing to tell others about You so they too will be saved. Amen.

Do not lie to each other. Colossians 3:9

To Tell the Truth

"What's a lie?" Mr. Costello asked his class.

"Something that isn't true," answered Martin.

"Like a fairy tale or a parable?" asked Mr. Costello.

"No, that wouldn't be a lie. A lie is … well, maybe I don't know. What is a lie?" Martin asked and looked around at his classmates for help.

"You have to want to cheat people or hurt them," said Cassidy. "Then it's a lie."

"Like when you say, 'I'll come over right away,' but you don't mean it, that's a lie," said Kathy.

"Or if you say that something you want to sell is good when you know it isn't," said Laura.

"Or even if you say, 'Paul told a lie,' and you think he did, but he didn't," said Allan.

"Or when you say that all people go to heaven and don't need Jesus to save them, that's maybe the worst lie of all," said Marcus.

"Now you see that lying is hurting people by not telling the truth. It's especially bad when you know better and tell lies on purpose," said Mr. Costello. "God says in the Bible, 'Do not lie to each other.' And why shouldn't we lie?"

All the students knew that answer and raised their hands. "We belong to Jesus and want to be like Him, and He doesn't lie," said John.

"And because we love Jesus, we don't want to hurt other people," added Mr. Costello.

Let's talk: Why isn't a fairy tale a lie even though it didn't happen? What is a lie? When is a lie especially bad? What were some of the lies the students mentioned? What does the Bible verse say about lying? Why shouldn't we lie?

Older children and adults may read: Colossians 3:9–15

Let's pray: Father in heaven, please forgive all the lies with which we have hurt people. Help us speak the truth in love and follow Jesus' example. In His name we ask it. Amen.

"Do not swear at all. … Simply let your 'Yes' be 'Yes,' and your 'No,' 'No.' " Matthew 5:34, 37

When "Yes" and "No" Are Enough

"I'll bring it right back," said Dallas. "Cross my heart and hope to die." He was promising to bring Shawn Simmon's new bike back as soon as he had tried it out.

Shawn's dad was standing near Dallas and heard what he said.

"Dallas, when you promise to bring something back, we believe you. You don't have to cross your heart and hope to die," said Mr. Simmons.

"Is it wrong to say that?" asked Dallas. He could tell Mr. Simmons didn't like it.

"Would you like to hear what Jesus said about it?" asked Mr. Simmons. Dallas nodded yes.

Mr. Simmons took a little New Testament from his pocket and turned to Matthew 5. He read, "Do not swear at all. … Simply let your 'Yes' be 'Yes,' and your 'No,' 'No.' "

"You see, even long ago people said 'By heavens' or 'By Jerusalem.' But Jesus said, 'Don't do it. just say yes or no,' " explained Mr. Simmons. "If people won't believe you when you say yes, then they won't believe you when you say 'Yes, and cross my heart.' "

"One of our neighbors says 'By Jove.' Is that wrong?" asked Shawn.

"That isn't God's name," said Mr. Simmons. "But I think Jesus likes it better if we don't add anything to back up what we say. We might start using God's name without thinking of what we're saying."

Let's talk: What did Dallas say when he promised to return Shawn's bike? What did Jesus say about swearing? How did

He say we should answer people? Why does Jesus want us just to say yes and no?

Older children and adults may read: Matthew 5:33–37

Let's pray: Dear Father in heaven, please help us watch our words so that we don't say things that are wrong. Teach us to be careful and say only words that are helpful and kind, as Jesus would. In His name we ask it. Amen.

The way of a fool seems right to him, but a wise man listens to advice. Proverbs 12:15

Stubborn Samuel

We shouldn't call people names like Stubborn Samuel, but in a way, Samuel deserved his nickname.

"I think you'd better wear a jacket. It's cold outside," Mother told Samuel.

"Aw, I don't need a jacket," Samuel argued. So he went outside and caught a cold. He missed his class picnic because he wouldn't listen to his mother's advice.

"Write your 5 this way," Samuel's teacher showed him.

"I want to do it my way," Samuel said. He kept writing it backwards and got a D on his math test because the teacher didn't understand what he had written.

Samuel was foolish to think he was always right. His foolishness made him stubborn. The Bible says, "The way of a fool seems right to him, but a wise man listens to advice." We learn a lot when we listen to others.

That's true most of all when we do wrong. If somebody tells us we're wrong, we need to be willing to stop and think. If it's true, we need to change our behavior. And we can ask God to help us quit stubbornly doing the same sins over and over. He will help us for Jesus' sake.

Some people would rather be wrong than corrected. The Bible calls these people fools. Wise people think over what others tell them. Wise people listen to advice.

The biggest fools are people who think their ways are always right. They don't believe they need God's forgiveness and help. Wise people believe the Word of God and believe that Jesus is their Savior and helper.

Let's talk: What did people call Samuel? Why did he have that nickname? Why is it foolish to think that your way is always right? What does the Bible call a person who listens to advice? What advice does God give people who turn to Him for help?

Older children and adults may read: Psalm 119:9–12

Let's pray: Dear Lord, please keep us from thinking that we're always right and can't be wrong. Make us wise enough to learn from other people and especially from those who teach us Your Word. Keep us as Your dear children through Jesus Christ. Help us to gladly follow His ways. In Jesus' name we pray. Amen.

Serve one another in love. Galatians 5:13

The Best Neighbors

"I wonder why the new neighbors are so friendly and helpful," Mr. Stone said to himself. "Nobody does something for nothing." Mr. Stone was rich, and people were always asking him for money or favors.

But Mr. Stone's new neighbors, the Larsons, never asked for anything. In fact, they were always giving him something or were trying to help him.

One time Mr. and Mrs. Stone got back from a trip late at night. Mrs. Larson knew they probably didn't have anything to eat in their house. She brought them some soup and homemade bread and even some pie for dessert. Mr. and Mrs. Stone enjoyed her gift.

Another time, Mr. and Mrs. Stone's grandson came to visit. He was afraid to stay alone with the maid, so the Larsons invited him to play with their children during the day.

When Mr. Stone came to pick him up, he asked, "What's your charge?" Mr. Larson laughed and said there was no charge. They enjoyed helping people.

It took quite awhile, but Mr. Stone finally found out why Mr. and Mrs. Larson were so nice. They believed in Jesus and had God's love in their hearts. This love made them want to help others. Mr. Stone thought they were the best neighbors he could have.

When Mr. and Mrs. Larson started talking to Mr. Stone about Jesus one evening, he listened. He even told his wife about their talk later that night. Mr. and Mrs. Stone asked God to be a part of their hearts and home too.

The Bible says, "Serve one another in love." We can be the kindest, friendliest, happiest people on earth because Jesus helps us to be that way. His law is summed up in one sentence: "Love your neighbor as yourself." When His love is in our hearts, that's what we want to do.

≈

Let's talk: At first why did Mr. Stone think the Larsons were friendly? Why *were* they friendly? How did their friendliness help the Larsons tell Mr. and Mrs. Stone about Jesus? Why can we be the happiest and kindest neighbors? Memorize the Bible verse.

Older children and adults may read: 1 Corinthians 13:4–7

Let's pray: O Lord of love, please forgive the times we have been unfriendly and unkind. Help us always to act as Your children and to give the love to others that we receive through Your Son, Jesus. Amen.

Praise the LORD, O my soul, and forget not all His benefits.
Psalm 103:2

What Lorenzo Didn't Remember

Lorenzo had a toothache. He asked God to make the toothache go away. The next morning it was gone, so Lorenzo didn't think about it anymore. He even forgot that he had asked God to help him. And, of course, that meant he didn't thank God.

The next day was Lorenzo's birthday. "Please let me get a dog, dear God," he prayed that morning.

He didn't get a dog, but Lorenzo did get two pretty white rabbits. "I like them even better than a dog," said Lorenzo. But he forgot that God is the Giver of all good gifts, and he forgot to thank God.

Two days later, Lorenzo got grease all over his clothes.

His mother had told him to stay away from the engine his dad was fixing. "Please, God," Lorenzo prayed, "help me clean this off my clothes so Mom won't get angry."

Lorenzo didn't get the grease off his clothes, but his mother didn't get angry. She only asked Lorenzo to be more careful with his clothes. As usual, Lorenzo forgot to thank God for a mother who was kind and forgiving.

On Sunday Lorenzo's Sunday school teacher asked, "Do any of you remember how God had answered your prayers this past week?"

Some did. But Lorenzo said, "I don't think God answered any of my prayers."

Lorenzo didn't know how God had answered his prayers. He forgot how he had prayed. He also forgot to thank God for his blessings. That's why he didn't know how God answered his prayers.

The psalm writer said, "Praise the LORD, O my soul, and forget not all His benefits." We thank God especially for His forgiveness of our sins. God gladly gives His love every day to all who ask Him. So "Praise the LORD, O my soul, and forget not all His benefits."

Let's talk: What were some things Lorenzo prayed for? How did God answer his prayers? Why didn't Lorenzo notice that God answered his prayers? What does the psalm writer tell us not to forget? What gifts can we thank God for every day?

Older children and adults may read: Matthew 7:7–11

Let's pray: Dear God, please forgive the many times we forget to thank You for what You do for us. Help us notice Your blessings so that we will love and praise You. In Jesus' name we ask this. Amen.

In Christ we who are many form one body. Romans 12:5

One Big, Happy Family

The Nelson family bought a farm in Iowa. Soon after they moved to their new home, the neighbors came to welcome them. All the neighbors were nice people, but especially the Millers who seemed like old friends right from the start.

"I'm glad to see that picture of Jesus on your wall," Mrs. Miller said to Mrs. Nelson. "We believe in Him too, so that makes us relatives. Have you joined a church? We'll be glad to have you come to ours."

When everybody was gone, Mrs. Nelson told her husband, "Isn't it wonderful how quickly we feel at home with people who believe in Jesus like we do?"

"I was thinking the same thing," said Mr. Nelson. "It's like the time I was in the Army. I was always glad to find someone else who was a Christian. The love of Jesus draws His followers together."

"We learned a Bible verse about that in Sunday school," said their daughter Kimberly. "It said, 'In Christ we who are many form one body.' That means the church of Jesus is like our body. There are a lot of members or parts, but they're all connected to one head. Jesus is the Head of His Church."

"When people are Christians, you know a whole lot about them right away," agreed Mr. Nelson. "You know they love God and pray and want to obey God and a lot of other things. You really do feel related, like brothers and sisters in a big, happy family."

"That's why we want to worship and work together with other Christians," Mrs. Nelson added. "So where do you think we're all going Sunday?"

Let's talk: What did Mrs. Miller notice on the wall of the Nelson home? Why did the Nelsons and the Millers feel like old friends? What had Kimberly learned about Jesus' followers? What are some things we know about other Christians? Where do you think the Nelson family went the next Sunday?

Older children and adults may read: 1 Corinthians 12:12–27

Let's pray: Lord Jesus, we're glad You have made us members of Your family. Help us remember that all who believe in You are children of God and are our brothers and sisters. Please add more people to Your church so that they too may enjoy Your love and blessings as we do. Amen.

We brought nothing into the world, and we can take nothing out of it. 1 Timothy 6:7

What Good Is Money?

An old lady lived all alone in New York City. She was extremely rich, but she hid all her money and never used it to help anybody, not even herself.

The old woman died because she didn't even buy

enough food for herself. Her neighbors paid for her funeral. They thought she was poor.

When the police searched the woman's house to find out if she had any family, they opened a chest of drawers. It was full of money and bank papers. In a closet they found some boxes full of money.

What good did it do the woman to have so much money? Her relatives got it all when she died.

The Bible tells us, "We brought nothing into the world, and we can take nothing out of it." What God gives us for just awhile, He wants us to use in good ways. When God gives us more than we need, He wants us to help others. Money is good to have when we use it for what we need and for helping others.

Children as well as grown-ups need to learn how money ought to be used. Some people love money. Some waste it. Our money and everything else we have is given to us by God. His gifts are to be used for good reasons.

God also wants us to be satisfied and happy with what He gives us. We can be happy when Jesus is in our heart because we know that God loves us, no matter what He gives us.

Let's talk: Why did the old lady die? What good did her money do her? What are some wrong ways of using money? What does God want us to do with the money He gives us? What does our Bible verse say about money and other things we own? Why can we be happy with whatever God gives us?

Older children and adults may read: Matthew 6:19–21

Let's pray: Forgive us, dear heavenly Father, for often wanting to keep things selfishly for ourselves. Help us see how You want us to use our money and things. Make us glad to use them in ways that are pleasing to You. We ask this in Jesus' name. Amen.

Train a child in the way he should go. Proverbs 22:6

God's Baby-sitters

"Mommy, you must be God's baby-sitter," said Paul.

"What makes you think so?" asked Mother.

"Well, when Mrs. Hanson comes and takes care of me, she's your baby-sitter. So when you take care of me, you're God's baby-sitter, aren't you?" asked Paul.

"In a way, you're right," his mother said. "You're really God's child. Your daddy and I are just taking care of you for God while you're little."

"You're my best baby-sitter," said Paul as he gave his mother a hug.

"I'm glad you love me," said Mother. "What do you think God's baby-sitter should do for Him?"

After thinking hard, Paul smiled. "A baby-sitter should not let me do anything wrong. A good baby-sitter keeps an eye on me and also tells me what you want me to do," said Paul. "And I like it when she reads to me or plays and sings with me."

"Very good," said Mother. She was beginning to enjoy the idea of being a baby-sitter for God. "I sometimes leave notes for your baby-sitters. Do you know where God's notes are for His baby-sitters?"

"Sure," said Paul. "They're in the Bible. Is that why you read your Bible so often?"

"That's one reason," said Mother. "One of God's notes said to me last week, 'Train up a child in the way he should go.' What do you think that way is?"

"It's the way Jesus wants me to go," said Paul. "It's going with Him."

"That's right," said his mother. "Following Jesus is the way God wants us to go."

Let's talk: What did Paul call his mother? Why? What are some things a good baby-sitter does? What does God want parents to do for Him? Where did Paul's mother find her notes from God? What was the Bible note she told Paul?

Older children and adults may read: Matthew 18:1–6

Let's pray: Please, dear God, give everyone in our house the love of Jesus so that we will grow up loving Him and following Your ways. We ask this through Jesus Christ, our Lord. Amen.

[Jesus] is the one whom God appointed as judge of the living and the dead. Acts 10:42

When the Judge Is Your Friend

"And don't you ever do that again," said the angry policeman, "or I'll take you before Judge Horn, and he'll be tough on you."

Steven was sorry he had taken the pen from the store, but he said to himself, "The judge won't be tough on me. He comes to our house often, and he's my friend."

He wasn't afraid of the judge, and that's why the policeman's words didn't frighten him.

The Bible says, "[Jesus] is the one whom God appointed as judge of the living and the dead." Jesus is the ruler of the world. He is the one who will decide whether we should be punished for what we do wrong. He is the judge before whom everybody will have to stand.

But we can say, "I'm not afraid of the judge. He's my Friend. He's my Savior. He died for me on the cross."

Jesus, the judge of the world, died to pay for our sins. He knows that our fines are paid—He paid them Himself. We won't even have to remind Him. Because we believe in Him, our sins are forgiven and we aren't punished.

Isn't that a good thing to know? Even the devil can't scare us when Jesus, our judge, is our Friend. Don't forget to thank Jesus for that.

⌒

Let's talk: How did the policeman try to scare Steven? Why was Steven sure the judge would be kind to him? Who is the judge of all people? How do we know that the judge will be kind and forgiving to us? Why won't we have to pay for what we do wrong? How can we show that we appreciate Jesus' love and friendship?

Older children and adults may read: Romans 8:31–34

Let's pray: Dear Jesus, we're glad that You aren't only our judge but also our loving Savior and Friend. Please judge us as your friends and not as we deserve to be judged. Have mercy on us, dear Jesus, forgive our sins, and help us to praise and serve You in love. Amen.

But you were washed ... in the name of the Lord Jesus Christ. 1 Corinthians 6:11

How We Are Washed by Jesus

"Mommie, do I have to be washed in blood?" asked 7-year-old Marissa when she came home from Sunday school.

"No," said Mother. "Who told you that?"

"My Sunday school teacher," answered Marissa. "She wants us to be washed in Jesus' blood."

Erick, her older brother, snickered, but Mother gave him a stern look. "Your teacher didn't mean that you had to be washed with blood the way we wash with water," Mother told Marissa. "She meant that Jesus washes away your sins with His blood the way water washes away dirt."

"But how can He do that with His blood?" asked Marissa.

"When Jesus died on the cross," Mother explained, "He gave His blood for us. This means that He gave His life for us. He died for us. When we believe that Jesus is our Savior, His blood saves us because God forgives us."

"But why did Jesus have to die for us?" asked Marissa.

"Well, we think bad things and do a lot of bad things. We're not the people God wants us to be. Jesus died on the cross so we could have a new life with God," Mother explained.

"See the dirt on this potato?" asked Mother. "Now I'll wash it with water. See, it's clean. The water took the dirt away. The Bible says, 'The blood of Jesus ... cleanses us from all sin.' "

Let's talk: What did Marissa's Sunday school teacher tell her? What did Marissa think this meant? What does it really mean? Why did Jesus give His blood and life on the cross?

Older children and adults may read: Hebrews 9:11–15

Let's pray: Lord Jesus, we owe You so much for giving Your blood and Your life for us! Thank You for washing away all our sins. Give us the Holy Spirit so that we will live a clean life for You. Amen.

Anyone who breaks one of the least of these commandments and teaches others to do the same will be called least in the kingdom of heaven, but whoever practices and teaches these commands will be called great in the kingdom of heaven.
Matthew 5:19

Little Things That Matter

"Who cares?" replied Karen when her mother asked her to pick up the dolls on the living room floor. "Nobody's coming."

Mother stopped dusting. "I care," she said, "and I'm sure God cares. God wants you to obey your parents in little things as well as in big things."

"But, Mom," Karen argued, "what's the difference whether I do it now or afterwhile?"

"The difference is in your spirit," Mother said. "You see, with God little things sometimes matter the most. The person who obeys God in little things usually loves Him more than people who do just the big things."

Caring about God in little things is very important. That's what Jesus was trying to teach us when He said, "Anyone who breaks one of the least of these commandments and teaches others to do the same will be called least in the kingdom of heaven, but whoever practices and teaches these commands will be called great in the kingdom of heaven."

Sometimes people think it doesn't matter if we sin just a little. Or they think some of the things God has told us aren't important. But it's often in the little things we do that we show how little or how much we love God.

That's why Karen's mother was very happy when Karen picked up her dolls.

⌒

Let's talk: What did Karen think didn't matter? What did Mother tell her? Who will be called great in God's kingdom? What are some little ways in which we show our love for God?

Older children and adults may read: Matthew 5:17–20

Let's pray: Lord Jesus, please forgive us for not caring enough about what God's will is. Make us willing to please You in the little things that don't seem important to us. Help us show our love for You in all that we do, especially in the little things. Amen.

"Father, ... not My will, but Yours be done." Luke 22:42

We Might Be Wrong

Cameron and his sisters were eating in a fancy restaurant. Cameron looked at the card. He didn't know what all the words meant. "I think this looks good," he told the waiter. "But don't bring it if it isn't good."

"Me too," his sisters added. "Bring me what's good."

The children left it up to the waiter to bring what he thought was best. And they enjoyed what he brought. He even made them pink lemonade for a surprise.

That's how we ought to let God do things for us. We don't know what's best for us. The best we can do is let God decide. God's will is always better than our will because He knows much more than we do.

Even when it meant dying on the cross, Jesus told His

Father in heaven, "Not My will, but Yours be done." Jesus knew He had to suffer to save people from sin and hell. But He was willing to do it because Jesus knew that it was God's plan to save us.

Jesus taught His disciples to pray, "Our Father who art in heaven, … Thy will be done."

Whenever we let God decide what should be done, He does what's best for us. Even though God tells us to ask Him for what we want, it's always good to add, "But please do what You think is best."

Let's talk: Why did Cameron and his sisters let the waiter decide their order? How did it work out? How did Jesus pray to His Father in heaven? Why did He teach us to pray, "Thy will be done"? Why aren't we always willing to let God decide things for us? How do things turn out when we let God decide what should happen?

Older children and adults may read: Matthew 26:36–44

Let's pray: Lord Jesus, teach us to pray as You did and to trust our Father in heaven. Help us believe that all things work out for good for those who love God. Remind us often that our Father in heaven loves us for Your sake. Amen.

But godliness with contentment is great gain. 1 Timothy 6:6

How to Make a Great Profit

Do you know what a *profit* is?

Lamar's father bought a car for $5,000 and sold it for $6,000. He made a profit of $1,000. Mr. Roth was a farmer. He made extra money by feeding cattle and then selling them. What he gained was his profit.

Everybody wants to get a profit by what they do. We all want to make some money or get some good out of what we do. Some people want to make big profits fast so they can buy a big house and a new car and lots of fancy clothes and the best food. Some people even cheat to get money and things that money can buy.

There's a better way to make a great profit. When we get this profit, we gain a lot more than money or things. The Bible says, "But godliness with contentment is great gain."

There was a famous doctor who could have been a rich man. He could have lived in a big house. But he gave his time and money to a hospital in Africa. He was satisfied with a small house and hardly any money because he loved God and wanted to help others.

A teacher who lives in New Guinea could make money and have a more comfortable life in the United States. But she went to New Guinea to help the people there because she loves God. God makes her happier than she would be is she were rich. God blesses her in many other ways.

Those who are satisfied with God's love get the most out of life on earth. And think of the wonderful life with God they'll get in heaven!

>**Let's talk:** What does *profit* mean? What does the Bible say is the best way to get a great profit? Why can we be satisfied and happy when Jesus is our Friend and Savior? What are some of the profits that come from being satisfied with God's love?

Older children and adults may read: Acts 4:32–37

Let's pray: Lord God, our Father in heaven, please make us completely satisfied with the love that You give through Jesus Christ, our Lord. Give us the Holy Spirit so we will believe there is great profit in loving You. Give us joy in serving You. In Jesus' name we ask it. Amen.

Now is the day of salvation. 2 Corinthians 6:2

Our Time Is Now

Lorene took her neighbor Dirk to Sunday school and church with her every Sunday. She often had to wait for Dirk to get ready. While she waited, she talked to his dad or mom and invited them to church too.

"We'll come sometime," Dirk's dad would say. But he

didn't really mean it. "Maybe when we're older and don't have as much to do," Dirk's mom would add.

One Saturday when Lorene was playing at Dirk's house, she listened as a man tried to sell Dirk's dad some insurance.

"There's lots of time for me to buy insurance," said Dirk's dad. "I'm still young."

"Let me tell you something," said the insurance agent. "Yesterday one of my friends died. He was only 25 years old. He thought he would live to be 80. Nobody knows how long a person will live. We need to be ready."

"That's right," said Lorene, before she even knew what she was saying.

"Lorene lives next door," explained Dirk's dad. "She's been telling me to go to church. I say there's plenty of time for such things, but you say there isn't. Do you go to church?"

"Well, no, but I guess a person should," the insurance agent answered. The next week, Lorene saw the insurance agent at her church.

While we're living on earth, God offers to adopt us as His children for Jesus' sake. But don't put off living your life with God. We don't know how long God will let us live. Tomorrow may be too late because tomorrow may never come. The Bible says, "*Now* is the day of salvation."

⇐

Let's talk: What did Lorene tell Dirk's parents about church? What did they say? What happened to the insurance agent's friend? What does God mean when He says, "*Now* is the day of salvation"?

Older children and adults may read: 2 Corinthians 6:1–2, 16–18

Let's pray: Dear Lord, our God, please keep us from wanting to wait until some other time to be Your children. Make us glad that now is our chance to have Your love. Help us find ways to tell others that *now* is the time to live with Jesus in His kingdom. In His name we pray. Amen.

Go to the ant, you sluggard; consider its ways and be wise!
Proverbs 6:6

What the Ants Teach Us

"Why do I have to do the dishes? Miguel doesn't!" Isabella complained as she sat reading a book.

"Miguel cuts the lawn and keeps the weeds out of the flowers," answered her mother.

"I'll trade you, Isabella," said Miguel. "But then you'll have to do everything I do."

Isabella wasn't sure she wanted to trade because Miguel always seemed to be busy. She quit grumbling, but she wasn't happy as she helped clear the table.

Isabella's mother worried about her laziness. "Everybody needs to learn to work," she told Isabella. "I hope you'll learn to like work. Your life won't be very happy if you don't enjoy working."

"Enjoy work?" asked Isabella, surprised that anyone could enjoy working.

"You should watch the ants," suggested Miguel. "They're happy because they're busy. You'd be happier too if you weren't so lazy."

"Yes, the Bible tells us to go and watch how hard the ants work," Mother agreed. "They teach us not to be lazy."

Miguel kept his ant farm on the back porch. Isabella

went outside and took a good look at the ants hurrying to carry food or sand from one place to another. "Those ants certainly are busy," she said to herself. "I guess God wants us to work."

The Bible says, "Whatever your hand finds to do, do it with all your might." The ants are a good example of hard workers. That's why the Bible says, "Go to the ant, you sluggard; consider its ways and be wise!"

Let's talk: Why was Isabella's mother worried about her? Why did she want Isabella to learn to work? What did Miguel tell her to watch? What does the Bible say we can learn from the ant?

Older children and adults may read: Proverbs 6:6–11

Let's pray: Lord God, please forgive our laziness and keep us from being lazy. Help us enjoy work as well as play, and teach us to work for You. We ask this in the name of Jesus, who never got tired of working for others. Amen.

It is more blessed to give than to receive. Acts 20:35

More Fun than Getting

"Why, Jonathan, what's the matter?" asked his mother. "Why are you crying? I thought all these Christmas presents from your friends at school would make you happy."

Jonathan had pneumonia and wasn't allowed to get out of bed. His class at school had sent him a big sack of packages.

"I'm happy to get all these presents," said Jonathan, "but I wish I could go to school and give somebody else a present."

Jonathan knew that the Bible says, "It is more blessed to give than to receive." So he asked his mother to bake a big batch of cookies to send to his friends at school. Jonathan got more fun out of that than out of the presents he received.

What made Jonathan even happier was planning to give Jesus a present. "After all, Christmas is Jesus' birthday," he explained to his mom. "He gave His life for me, so I want to give Him a present."

Some people think they'll only be happy when they get things. "I want this" and "Can't I have that?" and "Gimme some more," they say. But often people who get the most are the least happy.

People who have Jesus in their hearts know about love. And those who know about the love Jesus gives want to give to others instead of always getting. Just remember what Jesus said, "It is more blessed to give than to receive."

Let's talk: What did Jesus say was better than getting? What was Jesus glad to give us? What made Him glad to give His life? Why was Jonathan glad to give a present to Jesus?

Older children and adults may read: Acts 20:32–35

Let's pray: Dear Jesus, please help us believe that "it is more blessed to give than to receive." Give us the Holy Spirit so that we will enjoy Your love and also share it with others. Amen.

You must rid yourselves of all … filthy language from your lips. Colossians 3:8

Where to Put Dirty Talk

The man was dressed in a clean white suit and looked nice. But when he spoke, dirty, bad words came out of his mouth.

God wouldn't care much if the man's clothes were dirty, but He does care about dirty talk. In the Bible, God says, "You must rid yourselves of all … filthy language from your lips." People who talk dirty have dirty thoughts.

We often like to say dirty words. We might think such words are funny or that saying them makes us big and tough.

One day Shane was caught writing dirty words on the bathroom wall. Mr. Mason was surprised because Shane said he was a Christian. "How can you think and talk like that if Jesus is in your heart?" asked Mr. Mason.

Shane didn't want to answer. He knew he had to ask Jesus to take the dirtiness from his mind and mouth. Because he loved Jesus, Shane said, "I'm sorry, and I'm ashamed of what I did. I'll wash off what I wrote."

"And don't forget to ask Jesus to forgive you," said Mr. Mason. "He'll help you avoid dirty thoughts and words. "

The apostle Paul told the Christians in Corinth that God would be their Father and they would be His sons and daughters. Then Paul wrote, "Since we have these promises, ... let us purify ourselves." This includes getting rid of all dirty words.

~

Let's talk: Why is a clean mouth more important than clean clothes? Why do some people like to say or write dirty words? Why was Mr. Mason surprised to find Shane writing dirty words? What did Mr. Mason ask Shane? Why didn't Shane want to answer? Who helps us avoid dirty words and thoughts?

Older children and adults may read: Colossians 3:1–8

Let's pray: Create in us clean hearts, O God. Wash away all dirty words from our minds and mouths. Please give us the Holy Spirit so that we will think only clean and good thoughts. We ask this through Jesus Christ, our Lord. Amen.

Give thanks in all circumstances. 1 Thessalonians 5:18

A Secret Way to Stay Happy

When Taylor broke Vanessa's doll, Vanessa didn't say one angry word. "Aren't you going to get angry?" Taylor asked, quite surprised.

"No, I have a secret way of staying happy," explained Vanessa. "I learned it from my mother. No matter what happens, I think of the good things I have. When I think of them, I thank God for them. Then I don't feel so bad about what I don't have."

Vanessa's mother heard what she said and was surprised. "I didn't know you got that secret from me," she said. "I found it in the Bible."

"Could I see it in the Bible?" asked Taylor.

"Sure," said Vanessa's mother. She got her Bible and showed Taylor where the verse was. She had it marked with blue highlighter so she could quickly see it when she came to that page. It said, "Give thanks in all circumstances, for this is God's will for you in Christ Jesus."

"Does God really want us to give thanks even when bad things happen?" Taylor asked. "Do you think He wants us to be thankful because I broke the doll?"

"Maybe not because you broke the doll," said Vanessa's mother, "but because God loves us and He blesses us with so many other good things. I'm sure He'll see that Vanessa gets another doll too."

"I wish I belonged to Jesus," said Taylor, "so I could be happy all the time."

"Oh, now I'm glad you broke the doll," said Vanessa. "You can belong to Jesus. He wants you to be one of His friends. You can come to Sunday school and church with me and get to know Him better."

So that's how Taylor learned about Jesus and His love. And by learning about Jesus, she soon found many reasons to give thanks in everything.

Let's talk: What surprised Taylor? What was Vanessa's secret way of staying happy? Why was Vanessa able to give thanks in everything? What made Vanessa glad that Taylor broke the doll? Can you think of something bad that turned out good for you? Memorize the Bible verse.

Older children and adults may read: Matthew 19:27–30

Let's pray: Dear Father in heaven, we're glad that You love us and won't let anything bad happen to us. Please help us remember Your love, especially when things go wrong for us. Give us the Holy Spirit so we will give thanks in everything. In Jesus' name we ask it. Amen.

Do everything in love. 1 Corinthians 16:14

The Wheel That Caused Trouble

Once there was a beautiful car with four shiny wheels. The four wheels had a good time going places as long as they obeyed the steering wheel and went together.

But one day, one of the wheels decided to do what it wanted to do without caring about the other wheels. When the steering wheel told it to turn right, it turned left. This jerked the other wheels and stopped the car. A truck had to come and take it to a garage.

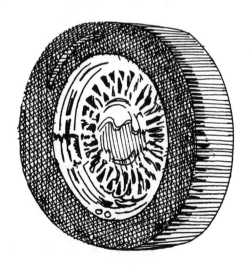

When the wheel saw the trouble it had caused, it was sorry and wanted another chance. So after it was straightened out, it didn't think only of itself anymore. Instead, it helped the other wheels go where the steering wheel wanted them to go together.

Sometimes we think we can do what we want. When we do what we want without caring about what happens to others, we cause a lot of trouble and usually hurt ourselves too.

The Bible says, "None of us lives to himself" nor by himself. There are always other people besides us who are hurt or blessed by what we do.

To keep us going places together with those around us, we need a steering wheel. The best steering wheel we can have is Jesus, our Lord and Savior. He tells us in the Bible, "Do everything in love." Love is caring about the people around us—caring about what will happen to them.

Jesus cared about what would happen to us. That's why He obeyed His Father in heaven and died on a cross for us. Now He wants us to care about others because we have His love in our hearts.

And here's a wonderful secret: Caring about other people makes us happy too.

Let's talk: When did the wheels of the car roll along happily? What happened when one of the wheels decided to disobey the steering wheel? Who is our steering wheel? How do we know that Jesus loves us? What's the main reason we have for loving other people?

Older children and adults may read: Romans 14:7–13

Let's pray: Dear Father in heaven, forgive us for often causing trouble by not loving others and by wanting our own way. Please give us the Holy Spirit so we will love You and those around us in all that we do. This we ask for the sake of Jesus, who loved us and died for us. Amen.

The fruit of the light consists in all goodness. Ephesians 5:9

The Nicest Gift

On the last day of classes before the Christmas holiday, the second grade at Bethel School had a Christmas party. All the children except one brought a present for the teacher. Reiko was the only student who didn't have a present. Her family didn't have a lot of money.

As Reiko sat and watched the other children take their presents to the teacher, she felt like crying. What would the teacher think of her? She wished she had something to give to show her love.

Then she got an idea and marched up to her teacher's desk. "Miss Rowan," she said, "I didn't have any money to buy you a present, but if I'm good all day, will that be nice enough?"

Miss Rowan looked at Reiko with a smile. "That would be the nicest gift of all," she said, and she meant it.

Reiko wanted to give Miss Rowan something because she loved her teacher. We love God because He first loved us and gave us His Son, Jesus. Jesus gave His life for us and gives us the Holy Spirit. Because God loves us, it makes us happy to give Him our love in return.

Obeying God is one of the nicest gifts we can give Him to show our love. God wants us to obey His commands and do good. He makes us want to do good when Jesus puts the Holy Spirit into our hearts. The Bible says, "The fruit of the light consists in all goodness." Being good shows that the Holy Spirit is in us.

~

Let's talk: Why did Reiko feel like crying at the school Christmas party? What did she ask Miss Rowan? What was Miss Rowan's answer? Why do God's children want to give Him gifts? When do our gifts please Him? What is the gift that pleases Him most?

Older children and adults may read: Ephesians 2:4–10

Let's pray: Dear Father in heaven, give us Your Holy Spirit so we can obey You and do good works. In Jesus' name we pray. Amen.

The Lord's servant must not quarrel; instead, he must be kind. 2 Timothy 2:24

The Missionary Who Argued

"I think I'll be a missionary," said Devon. "I like to argue religion."

"Devon's good at that," agreed his sister Marina. "You should hear him tell Adam off when Adam makes fun of going to church."

"Yeah, I gave him a piece of my mind when he said Sunday school was for the birds," Jevon bragged.

"Did you get him to go with you so he'll learn about Jesus?" asked Dad.

"No," Jevon admitted, "I haven't seen him since. He's avoiding me."

"You know," said Dad, "maybe you won the argument and lost Adam for Jesus."

"But aren't we supposed to speak for Jesus?" Devon argued.

"Yes," agreed Dad. "But Jesus didn't tell us to argue for Him. Do you know what He said we should be for Him?"

"I know," said Marina. "He said, 'You shall be My witnesses.' "

"What's the difference?" Devon continued to argue. "It's all the same."

"No, it isn't," said Marina. "A witness doesn't argue; a witness just tells what he knows and believes."

"I read a verse in the Bible last week that tells us not to argue, especially not when we speak for Jesus," Dad told them. "It says, 'The Lord's servant must not quarrel; instead, he must be kind.'

"See, Devon," Dad continued, "a missionary mustn't try to win *arguments* but *people*. When we argue too hard, it gets to be fighting, and then we lose people."

"All right," said Devon, "This week I'll try to win Adam for Jesus by being kind, and then we'll see."

Was Devon ever surprised! He treated Adam to an ice-cream cone and told him he was sorry about the way he had talked. "You're okay, Devon. Guess I'll go to Sunday school with you next Sunday," said Adam.

Let's talk: What did Devon want to be? What did he think missionaries had to do? What does Jesus want us to be for Him? Why is it better to win a person than an argument? Memorize the Bible verse.

Older children and adults may read: 2 Timothy 2:22–26

Let's pray: Please forgive our proud arguing, dear Lord. Help us to be kind so that we won't win arguments but people for You. In Jesus' name we pray. Amen.

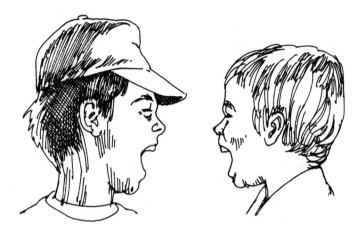

Better a patient man than a warrior. Proverbs 16:32

How to Become Strong

Quinn and Demond were arguing. Soon they were saying angry words. Then Quinn pushed Demond. Demond hit Quinn with a book.

Aunt Helena came into the room and stopped the fight. "Don't you remember what happened when Cain and Abel quarreled?" she asked them.

"It wasn't Abel's fault," said Quinn. He was trying to put the blame on Demond.

"Yeah, but you started this fight, and I'm going to finish it," said Demond, looking very angry.

"Demond," Aunt Helena said kindly, "God warned Cain when he became angry. He told Cain to watch out or he would do something he would regret. You know what happened? Out in the field Cain became so angry that he killed his brother."

"Aw, we weren't that angry," said Demond, a little ashamed.

"I hope not," said Aunt Helena. "You need to keep your temper down so it won't get worse as you grow older."

The Bible says, "Better a patient man than a warrior." In other words, people who can control their tempers are stronger than great fighters.

We can ask God to forgive our bad tempers and give us the power to control it. The Holy Spirit will give us the strength to remain patient. He will make us better than a mighty warrior.

Let's talk: What did Quinn and Demond's quarrel lead to? Why did Aunt Helena remind them of Cain and Abel? What happened when Cain lost his temper? What does the Bible say about the person who is slow to get angry and patient? Why is it bad to get angry easily? Who helps us control our tempers?

Older children and adults may read: Genesis 4:3–15

Let's pray: Dear Father in heaven, please forgive the many times we have gotten angry too quickly. Help us control our anger at all times so that we won't fall into even greater sins. We ask this in the name of Jesus, our Lord. Amen.

Whoever humbles himself will be exalted. Matthew 23:12

Stooping to Win

"You better watch out for that old man who moved into the house next to you," said David. "He looks mean, and he yells at kids."

Sure enough, one day Thomas ran too fast around the

 253

corner of his house and stepped on some of Mr. Wulff's flowers. Through the window Mr. Wulff saw what happened and came out yelling.

Thomas stopped. "I'm sorry I stepped on your flowers. I didn't watch where I was going. I'll ask my dad to plant some more flowers for you," Thomas said.

Mr. Wulff was surprised. He looked as though he didn't know what to say. Then he finally said, "You don't have to plant flowers there. I have plenty of flowers. I'm just a selfish old man."

After that Thomas became good friends with Mr. Wulff. Soon he was telling Mr. Wulff about his Sunday school lessons. Thomas always ended by talking about Jesus— how Jesus loved him and was with him and helped him. Mr. Wulff often asked Thomas questions about Jesus.

One day Thomas was extra happy. Mr. Wulff promised to go to church with Thomas and his family. The next Sunday Mr. Wulff was all dressed up and waiting on the porch when Thomas came to pick him up.

Eventually Mr. Wulff joined the pastor's instruction class and became a member of Thomas' church. Mr. Wulff believed that Jesus was his Savior.

How did Thomas get to be a good salesman for Jesus?

By being polite and friendly. He was willing to admit his mistakes and was humble. That's how God made Thomas a big success in winning people for Him and His church.

≈

Let's talk: How was Thomas humble when Mr. Wulff yelled at him? What did Mr. Wulff say when he saw that Thomas was sorry? How did God make Thomas a big success? Why was Mr. Wulff willing to listen to Thomas talk about Jesus?

Older children and adults may read: Matthew 23:1–12

Let's pray: Dear Father in heaven, please make us willing to be humble so that You can make us successful. Please make us a great success, especially in leading others to You. We ask this through Jesus Christ, our Lord. Amen.

We are God's workmanship, created in Christ Jesus to do good works. Ephesians 2:10

Created for Good Works

Mrs. Jasmine broke her leg when she fell down the steps. After she got back from the hospital, she wasn't sure how she'd get around. She lived by herself.

Before she even got her coat off, Liana and Samantha came over. They had seen Mrs. Jasmine get out of the taxi and had decided to help her.

"What would you like for dinner?" Liana asked. "I'm going to make it for you."

"Here, let me help you get that coat off so you can sit down," said Samantha, bringing a chair.

"You shouldn't be doing this," said Mrs. Jasmine, even though she was happy that the girls had come.

"Of course we should," said Samantha. "That's what we were made for."

Liana caught on right away. "Sure," she said with a twinkle in her eye. "God made us His children so we could help you when your leg was broken."

At first Mrs. Jasmine thought the girls were joking. "Do you girls really believe that?" she asked.

"Yes, Mrs. Jasmine," answered Samantha seriously. "God saved us and made us His children so we would do good works. That's what the Bible says."

"Well, that's amazing," said Mrs. Jasmine. "I thought you were saved by faith, and that it didn't matter whether you did good things."

"The Bible does say we are saved by grace, through faith in Jesus," Liana agreed. "But God makes us His children so we'll do good works. Right now we want to do some good right here, if you'll let us."

"Simply amazing," sighed Mrs. Jasmine again as she sat down to watch the girls enjoy helping her.

≈

Let's talk: Why did Liana and Samantha come over to Mrs. Jasmine's house? What did they tell Mrs. Jasmine? Why did she think the girls were joking? What wrong idea did Mrs. Jasmine have about faith and good works? What does the Bible verse say is God's reason for making us His children?

Older children and adults may read: Ephesians 2:4–10

Let's pray: Dear Father in heaven, we're thankful that You have made us Your children through faith in Jesus. Help us to be the most useful people we can be. Give us the Holy Spirit so that we will gladly do whatever we can to help others. In Jesus' name. Amen.

"Do not worry, saying, 'What shall we eat?' or 'What shall we drink?' or 'What shall we wear?' " Matthew 6:31

How to Worry Less

Adrian and his dad were looking at some plaques in a greeting card store. The plaques had sayings on them.

"Look at this one, Adrian," said Dad. "I think I'll buy it for our home. It may help us."

Adrian looked at the plaque. It said, "Why worry when you can pray?"

"Yes, sir," said Dad. "If we'd pray more, we wouldn't worry quite so much, that's for sure."

When they showed Mom the plaque, she said, "I know I need that little reminder. Whenever we get company, I worry about what to serve them. I worry about our bills and about my children and about getting my work done. Guess I'll have to pray more."

As they were talking, Vianna came into the room. She was going to a youth group party at church. "Mother," she said, "there's a spot on my dress, and I can't wear it. What'll I wear? I don't have anything to wear. It's awful."

Adrian showed Vianna the plaque, which said, "Why worry when you can pray?" At first it made Vianna angry. Then she laughed and said, "If I'd talk to God about my dress, I'm sure it wouldn't seem to matter much. I do have other dresses."

Jesus said, "Do not worry, saying, 'What shall we eat?' or 'What shall we drink?' or 'What shall we wear?'" People who have Jesus in their hearts find that there's not much to worry about. They always have enough food and clothing or anything else they really need.

Let's talk: What was on the plaque that Adrian's father bought? What does the saying mean? Why did Dad buy the plaque? What did Adrian's mom worry about? What was Vianna worried about? How did the plaque help her? Memorize the Bible verse.

Older children and adults may read: Matthew 6:31–34

Let's pray: Dear Father in heaven, we thank You for promising to take care of us. Help us trust You for all the things we really need so we will pray to You instead of worrying. In Jesus' name we ask it. Amen.

The whole earth is full of [God's] glory. Isaiah 6:3

A World Full of God's Wonders

The boys were lying on the floor, looking at a new book their mother had just bought them.

"Look, Mother," said Wade. "We don't see with our eyes in the front of our head. We see in the back with the brain!"

"And do you know something else about our eyes?"

said his brother Alec. "There are lots of tiny wires going from the eye to the brain. That's how we see."

"Not real wires," explained Wade, who had read a lot about people's bodies. "They're called nerves. Nerves are muscle wires."

"Only God could have made our wonderful bodies," said Mother. "Our eyes and the way they work are a miracle."

Then the boys turned to a different page in the book and read some more.

"Do you know how strong atoms are?" Alec asked. He could hardly believe what he was reading. "Atoms are real tiny. There are a million atoms in one peanut. But the atoms in one peanut could push a train from New York to Los Angeles. It says so right here."

"Don't forget that God put the power in the atom," Mother reminded the boys. "He put it there when He made the earth and all that's in it. How great God is and how wonderful His works are!"

The prophet Isaiah knew how great God is. He heard the angels of God saying to one another: "Holy, holy, holy is the Lord Almighty. The whole earth is full of His glory." God's greatness and glory can be seen in everything He made.

But even more wonderful is what God did for us when He sent His Son, Jesus, to save us from our sins. God's Son became a baby. Jesus was God's Son living on earth as a man. Jesus has "all power in heaven and on earth." He has the power "to save all who draw near to God through Him." That's how great God is!

Let's talk: What did Wade and Alec find out about their eyes? Why did Mother call this a miracle? How strong is an atom? Who gave the atom its power? What did Isaiah hear the angels say? What is even more wonderful than the world God has made?

Older children and adults may read: Isaiah 6:1–7

Let's pray: Dear Lord, we thank and praise You for the way You created us and the whole earth. But we love You most because You love us even though we are sinful. You even sent Your Son, Jesus, to die for us. We praise and thank You, O Lord, especially for that. Amen.

I will trust and not be afraid. Isaiah 12:2

Because God Is Near

Sydney was afraid to be alone in her upstairs bedroom without a light. So her mother tied a string to the switch and hung the string by her bed. Now Sydney could pull the string and turn the light on or off.

Then her mother told Sydney a story. "Once there was a little girl who was lost in the woods. When night came and it was dark, she started to cry. Then something rubbed against her leg. It was her dog. The girl was so happy to have her dog with her that she quit crying. A little later her father found her. Then the girl wasn't afraid anymore."

"I'm not afraid when Daddy is with me," said Sydney.

"God is our Father in heaven," said Mother, "and He's always near us. And so is His Son, Jesus. People who know Jesus loves them say, 'I will trust and not be afraid.' "

"I know Jesus loves me," said Sydney. "But how can I learn to trust Him?"

"Why do you trust me?" asked Mother.

"Because you come when I need you and call you," answered Sydney.

"Jesus is always closer to you than I can be," Mother explained. "He said, 'I am with you always.' He can do much more for you than I can."

Sydney thought about this for a few moments. "Mother, I'll turn the light off when you go," she finally said.

When her mother left, Sydney said to Jesus, "I will trust and not be afraid." Then she pulled the string, and soon she was fast asleep.

Let's talk: What story did Mother tell Sydney? Why? What made the lost girl feel safe? Why did Sydney trust her mother? Why can we trust God? Why was Sydney willing to go to sleep without a light? Memorize the Bible verse.

Older children and adults may read: Isaiah 12:1–6

Let's pray: Dear loving Father in heaven, please forgive us for not always trusting You. Make us brave and happy. Remind us that Jesus, our Savior, is always near us and loves us. In Jesus' name we ask it. Amen.

They gave themselves first to the Lord. 2 Corinthians 8:5

What Jesus Wants from Us

Adriana's family was very rich. But she seldom saw her parents. While they traveled all over the world, Adriana was left at home with the housekeeper.

One day Adriana's mother sent her a beautiful and expensive doll. At first Adriana didn't even want to open the package. When she saw the present, she threw the doll on the floor and broke it. Why do you think she did that?

Sobbing, Adriana cried, "Mother, don't just send me pretty things. I want *you!*" She cried for a long time.

Jesus also isn't satisfied when people give Him only things. Some people think He's pleased when they give His church a present now and then or when they give one of His children a gift. But Jesus wants *us*—our hearts, our love, ourselves.

The first Christians helped others all the time, even though they were poor. Can you guess why? The Bible says, "They gave themselves first to the Lord."

How do we give ourselves to the Lord? By believing that He is our Lord and Savior, by trusting His promises, by being thankful, by letting Him rule us and own us, by living with Him and for Him, and by listening to what He tells us in His Word.

Have we given ourselves to Jesus? He wants *us*, not just some presents. He even died on the cross so He could have us.

⌒

Let's talk: What made Adriana think her parents didn't love her? Why did Adriana break the present her mother sent? Why isn't Jesus satisfied when people give Him only things? What does the Bible say the first Christians gave to the Lord? How do we give ourselves to Jesus?

Older children and adults may read: 2 Corinthians 8:1–5

Let's pray: Dear Lord, we love You, but our love sometimes gets very small and cold. Please keep us from giving You anything without also giving You our heart. Amen.

Do to others what you would have them do to you.
Matthew 7:12

A Voice That Comes Back

Troy, who lived in the city, and his parents visited some relatives who lived on a farm. The first morning on the farm Troy got up early and took a walk by himself. It felt good to be out in the fresh air and the open spaces.

Out in a field, Troy began running like a horse. When he came to a woods, he stopped and shouted "Whoa!" to himself. Back came a voice that said "Whoa!" It sounded almost like Troy's.

Troy was surprised. He thought a boy was hiding among the trees. "Shut up!" yelled Troy. "Shut up!" the voice repeated. This made Troy angry. "I'll punch you in the nose!" he yelled. "I'll punch you in the nose!" said the voice.

Troy ran back to the house to tell his parents. "Mom," he said, "there's a mean boy in that woods. Whatever I say, he says. When I told him to shut up, he yelled, 'Shut up!' "

Mother laughed. "Troy, that voice was your echo. It said only what you said," she explained. "If you had called kind words into the woods, the voice would have answered you in a kind way."

"I hope you'll learn a lesson from this," said Troy's dad, who had been listening. "Other people usually treat us the way we treat them. Jesus gave us the Golden Rule. It tells us the way God wants us to treat other people. Do you remember it?"

"Yeah," answered Troy. "Do to others what you would have them do to you."

"That's right," said Dad. "When we follow this rule, we love others the way we would like to be loved. Then that love usually comes back to us."

"Of course, we all need a lot of help and practice in following the Golden Rule," said Mother. "But Jesus makes us willing and able. His voice in us is a loving voice. Why don't you go back to the woods and try the echo once more?"

So, just for fun, Troy ran back to the woods and yelled, "Let's be friends." At once the echo shouted back, "Let's be friends."

Let's talk: What did Troy hear when he yelled "Whoa!"? What did he think the echo was? What lesson did Troy's dad want him to learn? Who makes us willing and able to follow the Golden Rule? What good reasons do we have for practicing this rule? Memorize the Bible verse.

Older children and adults may read: Luke 6:27–31

Let's pray: Dear Lord Jesus, we're sorry that we don't always love others the way we want to be loved. Please forgive us and help us do to others what we would want them to do to us. Help us make our echo sound like You so that Your love will speak through us and will come back to us in what we say and do. Amen.

You shall not misuse the name of the LORD your God.
Exodus 20:7

What Can You Do?

Blake often went to his father's store on days when he didn't have school. His father told him that someday the store would be his, so he wanted to learn the business.

One day one of the workers told Blake, "You'll never amount to much, you're too small."

Blake answered, "I can do something you can't do."

"Oh?" replied the worker. "What?"

"I don't think I should tell you," said Blake.

But the worker was curious and begged Blake to tell. Finally, Blake said, "I can keep from swearing, and you can't."

The worker was ashamed. He knew he often said God's name without a good reason, and he knew this was wrong. But, like a lot of other people, the worker had gotten into the habit of cursing and swearing and no longer noticed it himself.

God commands, "You shall not misuse the name of the LORD your God." We are to love God so much that we won't curse or swear or use God's name without a good reason.

In the Bible, the apostle Paul said, "Whatever you do, do it all for the glory of God." Cursing and swearing dishonors God and never adds to His glory.

Instead of misusing God's name, we use His name to pray, to tell others about Him, and to give thanks to Him. Because we don't do this nearly enough, we're glad that God loves us and forgives us for Jesus' sake.

Let's talk: What could Blake do that a worker in his father's store couldn't do? How did the worker feel when Blake told him this? What made the worker feel that way? Which commandment forbids us to misuse God's name? What are some good ways of using God's name?

Older children and adults may read: Philippians 2:5–13

Let's pray: Dear Lord God, please forgive us the times we have used Your name in vain by saying it without talking to You or thinking about You. Keep us from using Your holy name for cursing and dirty talk or for no good reason at all. Help us keep Your name holy and use it to pray and praise You. We ask this in Jesus' name. Amen.

Love must be sincere. Romans 12:9

How Real Love Shows Itself

When Stacey was sick, her brother, Terry, did many favors for her. But when she was better, he stopped being as nice.

"Terry, why can't you be as nice to Stacey now as you were when she was sick?" Mother asked him one day. "I thought you told me you loved her."

"Sure I do," said Terry, "but Stacey knows that without me being nice to her all the time."

"But are you loving her when you aren't nice to her?" Mother asked. "Real love always shows itself. It's not enough just to say you love someone."

"You mean I can't love a person without doing something for her?" Terry asked.

"Not without wanting to do something for the person you love," Mother told him. "Tell me, did Jesus show His love for people?"

"Yes, He did," Terry admitted.

"Believe me," said Mother, "if your love is real, it will show. It will show itself in what you do."

"Okay," said Terry, and he decided he would try to love people by what he said and did. Terry started saying please and thank you. He tried to be more friendly and unselfish to Stacey.

One day Stacey told Terry, "You're the nicest brother I could have."

"And our home is so much happier since you decided to show your love," added Mother.

The Bible says, "Love must be sincere." It isn't sincere unless it's willing to act. Sincere love shows itself in loving behavior, just as Jesus showed His love in what He did.

Let's talk: When was Terry nice to Stacey? What wrong idea did Terry have when Stacey was better? What did Mother tell Terry? How did Jesus show His love for us? What kind of love does God want us to show?

Older children and adults may read: John 15:12–17

Let's pray: Dear heavenly Father, please help us have a sincere love for other people, especially for those in our home. Forgive us the many times we haven't shown love to others. Help us remember that real love shows itself in loving words and deeds. Give us the Holy Spirit so we will show love in whatever we do, through Jesus, who loved us and gave Himself for us. Amen.

May the favor of the Lord our God rest upon us. Psalm 90:17

The Beauty That Comes from God

Aileen was a little girl who wanted to be beautiful. "I wish I were pretty," she often said to herself. "Then people would love me more." So she combed and combed and combed her hair and wore pretty clothes and tried to smile and hold her head like a queen.

On a vacation in New Orleans, Aileen and her parents visited the streets where artists paint outside. "Please let the man paint a picture of me," Aileen begged. She thought the painter would make her look prettier than she was.

Her father agreed, so while the man painted her picture Aileen sat as straight and still as she could. "Please make it as pretty as you can," she asked. "If it isn't pretty, I don't want it." The painter smiled and told her she would be as pretty as a picture.

The painter made Aileen look very pretty, because he wanted her to be pleased with his painting. But when he was finished, her father said, "I don't want that picture. It doesn't look like my girl at all. You've made her too pretty."

Aileen began to cry. She wanted so much to be like the girl in the picture. Then her father took her in his arms and said, "Sweetheart, you don't have to pretend to be prettier than you are. You are the dearest girl in the world to me, so why should I want a picture that doesn't look like you?"

When Aileen heard that her father loved her because she belonged to him, his love seemed much more important than looking pretty. This made Aileen happy, and she also became more beautiful.

God, our Father in heaven, loves us. He loves us so much that He let His Son, Jesus, die for us on a cross. He wants us to be His children. He doesn't care how we look on the outside. All He wants is our love. When we love Him, His love makes us beautiful. That's why the psalm writer said, "May the favor of the Lord our God rest upon us."

Let's talk: What was Aileen worried about? Why did Aileen want her picture painted? Why didn't her father like the

painting? What did he tell Aileen when she started to cry? How did his love make Aileen feel? How is God like Aileen's father? Memorize the Bible verse.

Older children and adults may read: Psalm 90:14–17

Let's pray: Dear Father in heaven, help us remember that it's much more important to be pretty on the inside than on the outside. Make us beautiful by filling our hearts with Your love, through Jesus Christ, our Lord. Amen.

We have different gifts according to the grace given us.
Romans 12:6

Different Kinds of Gifts

"Akiko knows hardly anything in school," said Sherisa one evening. "She's so dumb."

"Akiko held the organist's baby in church last Sunday," her mother answered. "I noticed some other girls sitting there who didn't help."

"You mean me, don't you, Mom," said Sherisa, blushing a little. "I was talking about knowing things."

"Knowing how to help someone and how to make a baby happy is knowing quite a bit," Mother explained. "You see, God has made every person different. We all have gifts from God that differ according to what He has given us. That's what the Bible tells us. We can't all be good in knowing lessons and books."

"Like our coach," agreed Sherisa's brother Brett. "He knows how to make boys quit fighting and be friends."

"That's knowing how to be a peacemaker," said Mother. "Mateo, who tries hard in math but just can't catch on, is the best lifeguard I know."

"That's right," said Brett.

"So you see, Sherisa," Mother repeated, "just knowing things out of books isn't the only kind of knowing. Maybe we should learn this verse from the Bible to help us remember what we've talked about: 'We have different gifts according to the grace given us.' Grace is the love and blessing of God."

They all said the verse together, and Sherisa decided she had learned a good lesson.

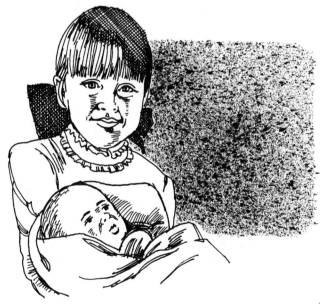

Let's talk: What didn't Akiko know very well? What was she good at? What are some people that you know good at? What does the Bible verse say we all have from God? What does God want us to do with whatever gifts He gives us?

Older children and adults may read: Romans 12:3–10

Let's pray: Thank You, dear Lord, for the gifts You have given us. Please keep us from being proud of what You give us. Help us remember that different people have different gifts from You. Give us the Holy Spirit so we will use our gifts to serve You and other people as well as we can. We ask this in Jesus' name. Amen.

I have you in my heart. Philippians 1:7

Pittakos Was Wrong

"You mark my words," said Pittakos, the pottery maker in the city called Philippi, "that fellow Paul is planning to cheat somebody. He wouldn't preach and go around doing good things just for nothing. Nobody does."

"You could be wrong," said Philip, the saddle maker next door. "This Paul says he does it for one who is called Jesus. He says that Jesus is God and that this Jesus went about doing good when He lived on earth. He says this Jesus wants His disciples to do only good to other people."

"Nobody loves anyone but himself," said Pittakos. "Even those who say they love God or their neighbor are trying to get something for themselves."

But Pittakos was wrong. Even though the first part of the story was made up, Paul did go to Philippi. There some people believed what He told them about Jesus. Others hated him and told lies about him. Some were sure his preaching was a trick to make money.

When Paul later wrote a letter to the Christians in Philippi, he told why he went to so much trouble to preach the Gospel to them. "I have you in my heart," he wrote. This meant, "I love you." He said he wanted the Philippians to get the blessings of Jesus and to grow to be good people.

Every pastor who loves Jesus feels as Paul did. He's willing to do even difficult things for people. Pastors tell others about Jesus' love and help them learn what God expects of them. Our pastor also says to us, "I have you in my heart."

Parents do a lot for their children because they have them in their hearts. That means they love them. And parents who love Jesus want their children to have His love so they'll become more and more like Him.

Do you have anyone in your heart? See if you can think of someone who doesn't know Jesus. Talk about ways you can show that person the love of our Lord. If that person wants to know why you're being nice, say, "I have you in my heart."

Let's talk: What did Pittakos think was Paul's reason for preaching in Philippi? What did Paul say was his reason? Who are some of the people teaching us the Word of God? What do you think is their reason for doing it? How can we be like Paul?

Older children and adults may read: Philippians 1:3–11

Let's pray: Dear God, we thank You for people like Paul, who spread the Good News about Jesus. Please open our hearts to others that we may love them and help them grow in Jesus' love. In His name we ask it. Amen.

The LORD is my Shepherd. Psalm 23:1

When the Good Shepherd Calls

In the beautiful country of Scotland, there was a shepherd who had a little daughter. Often he would take her with him when he led his sheep to green pastures or to pools of fresh water in the valleys.

The little girl loved to be with her father and his sheep. Most of all she liked to hear him call his sheep and see the sheep come when he called.

When the girl became a young woman, she went away to work in a big city. At first she wrote to her father every week, but soon the time between letters became longer and longer. Finally, she stopped writing altogether.

One day a young man from her village saw her in the big city and spoke to her. She acted as though she had never seen him before. Later some other people told him that she often got drunk and lived with men who weren't married to her.

When the young man returned home, he told the shepherd what he had heard about his daughter. At once the shepherd went to the city to look for her. Day after day he walked up and down the streets of the big city, hoping to find her.

Then he remembered how his little girl used to listen to him call his sheep. So he went through the streets of the city again, this time giving his shepherd's call.

When the daughter heard her father's voice, she knew at once who it was. Quickly she ran out to the street to find him. When they met, he took her into his arms and asked her to go back home with him. Because she saw how much he loved her, she went back with him.

Jesus said, "I am the Good Shepherd." We are His sheep. He even gave His life to save His sheep. His sheep know His voice. It's a forgiving, inviting voice, which His sheep love to hear and gladly follow.

"The LORD is my Shepherd," we say in Psalm 23. Jesus calls us away from our sins and leads us back to a beautiful life with God. His love makes us glad to go with Him.

Let's talk: What did the little girl enjoy hearing? What happened when she left her father and went to the big city? How did her father find her? Why did she go back home with him? Who is our Shepherd? Why is He called the Good Shepherd?

Older children and adults may read: Psalm 23

Let's pray: Dear Jesus, we're glad that You love us and that You are our Good Shepherd. Whenever we leave You by doing wrong or forgetting You, please call us by Your love to follow You. Amen.

Why not rather be wronged? Why not rather be cheated?
1 Corinthians 6:7

When It's Better to Lose

Christopher and Tad were arguing at the breakfast table. Over what? Over a little cardboard picture from the cereal box.

"Give it to me," said Christopher. "It's mine. You got the last one."

"I saw it first," said Tad, "and I'm keeping it."

"Why argue over a piece of paper?" Aimee asked them. "Is it worth a fight?"

"Well, Tad shouldn't be selfish," replied Christopher.

"Yeah, and you shouldn't be selfish either," said Tad, and that just about started the fight all over again.

Then Mother sat down to talk to them. "Boys," she said, "once many of the Christians in Corinth were arguing. They said nasty things about each other. They even went to the judges of the city and asked them to punish the Christians with whom they quarreled. Do you know what the apostle Paul told them?"

"He told them to quit fighting," Christopher guessed.

"Yes, he did," Mother said. "Paul told them, 'When you have a fight, you've already lost more than the fight.' Can you guess what that might mean?"

Both boys thought awhile. "Well, it might mean your temper has taken away your happy feelings," said Tad.

"And it might mean that when you argue, you could lose your friends and your friendship with God," added Christopher.

"Right," said Mother. "That's why the apostle Paul wrote, 'Why not rather be wronged? Why not rather be cheated?' So what do you think he'd say to you, Christopher?"

"I suppose Jesus would say, 'Christopher, why don't you let Tad have that picture? You'll lose something more important by fighting,' " Christopher admitted, a little ashamed.

"Now you're thinking like Jesus wants you to think," said Mother. "And Tad, you might lose your selfishness if you let yourself be cheated rather than fight and cheat. I'm sure God would prefer that. What do you think?"

Without doing anymore thinking, Tad handed the picture to Christopher and said, "Here's your card, Chris. I'm sorry I was selfish."

Let's talk: What were Christopher and Tad arguing about? Why wasn't the card worth a fight? What makes people argue over almost nothing? What did the apostle Paul tell some arguing Christians? What might Christians lose if they fight?

Older children and adults may read: 1 Corinthians 6:7–11

Let's pray: Dear heavenly Father, please forgive all the arguments and the mean words that have come from our selfish hearts. Give us the Holy Spirit so we will take wrong rather than do wrong, and be cheated rather than cheat. Help us become what You want us to be, for the sake of Jesus, who died to save us. Amen.

When you ask, you do not receive, because you ask with wrong [reasons]. James 4:3

When God Says No

Once some people asked an old man who was a Christian to ask God for rain. They knew this man prayed a lot. Before he prayed, the man asked what day would be best for rain.

Some of the women didn't want it to rain on Monday because that was their washday. They liked to hang their clothes outside to dry instead of putting them in the dryer. On Tuesday the people who went to the lake and those who had planned a picnic wanted clear weather. On Wednesday the farmers were going to cut their hay, and

on Thursday they wanted the hay to dry. On Friday there was a ballgame, and on Saturday many city people wanted to work in their yards and gardens. On Sunday, of course, the ministers didn't want rain to keep people from coming to church.

There was no day that suited everyone, so the man asked the Lord to send the rain whenever He thought it best, and that's the way He sends it.

This is just a story, but what it teaches is true. Sometimes we pray for good weather because we have something planned. When we wake up the next morning and it's raining, we may think that God didn't hear our prayer or doesn't care about us.

But God cares about all His people, and He does what is best for all. That's why He seldom answers a selfish prayer. A selfish prayer asks for things that may harm other people.

Think of what would happen if every day one person asked God to keep the rain from falling. If God always did what was asked, there wouldn't be anything to eat because food can't grow without rain.

The Bible says to people who pray selfish prayers, "When you ask, you do not receive, because you ask with wrong [reasons]." Jesus asked His heavenly Father, "Not My will, but Yours be done." From Jesus we learn to let God decide what's best for all when we pray. Then our prayers are always answered.

⟿

Let's talk: What did the old man ask before he prayed for rain? What did he find out? What did he finally ask the Lord to do? Why doesn't God answer selfish prayers? How did Jesus pray in Gethsemane before He died to save us from our sins? What can we learn from this prayer?

Older children and adults may read: Matthew 26:36–44

Let's pray:
> Dear Father, change my will today.
> Make it like Yours and take away
> All that now makes it hard to say,
> "Your will be done." Amen.

I know whom I have believed. 2 Timothy 1:12

It's Not What You Know

"Connor is real smart," said Shawna. "He's learning 600 Bible verses and where they are in the Bible. Next year I'm going to try to do that."

"He knows just about all of them," said Beth. "He said 50 last Sunday. It took almost the whole Sunday school hour to say them."

Shawna became a little jealous. "Mrs. Fraser was very proud of Connor, but you know what he did? He stole some money from the offering once," said Shawna.

"I wish you hadn't mentioned that," Beth gasped. "Connor said he was sorry, and he promised not to do it again. So let's not tell anybody, not anybody, ever again. Okay, Shawna?"

"I'm sorry," said Shawna, and she meant it because she knew she'd done wrong.

"Do you think you could know 600 Bible verses and not be a Christian?" Beth asked her father later that night.

"How many verses do you think the devil knows?" asked Dad.

"Oh, he probably knows them all," said Beth.

"That means just knowing Bible verses doesn't make anyone a Christian," explained Dad. "It's not *what* you know but *whom* you know that counts."

"That's right," said Beth's mother, who had been listening. "The apostle Paul told his friend Timothy, 'I know *whom* I have believed.' He didn't say, 'I know *what* I have believed.' He knew Jesus and believed Him. That's why he was a Christian."

Of course, it's good to know Bible verses because God talks to us through these words. And knowing Bible stories is good too, because they tell us about God's ways and God's people. But knowing that Jesus is our Lord and Savior is best of all. Believing that is what makes a person a Christian.

⁓

Let's talk: What was Connor learning? Why can a person know many Bible verses and still not be a Christian? What good is it to know Bible verses and Bible stories? What's most important of all? Why is knowing Jesus most important?

Older children and adults may read: 2 Timothy 1:8–12

Let's pray: Lord Jesus, we're glad that we know You and that You love us and are our Savior. Please keep us close to You until we're with You forever in heaven. Amen.

In [Jesus] we have ... the forgiveness of sins. Colossians 1:14

The Best Thing in the World

"Daddy, what is the worst thing in the world?" Renata asked one evening at the supper table.

"What do you think?" he asked.

"I think the worst thing in the world is being sick a long time and not being able to play outside," Renata answered.

"Good health is a great blessing, but people can be happy, even when they are sick," Dad said. "God often blesses His children through their sickness."

"I think the worst thing in the world is to be poor," said Renata's brother Stefano. And with a grin he added, "Could you raise my allowance, Dad?"

"God asks us to help people who are poor, but He has promised that His children will always have what they need. And He warns us against loving money. Maybe I should cut your allowance," Father replied with a smile.

"I think not getting an education is the worst trouble a person could have," said Francisco, who was a freshman in college. "People who don't learn much might not be able to get a job and take care of themselves."

Dad nodded in agreement. "A good mind and a good education are important blessings," he said. "But there are many happy and successful people who have had very little education."

"I know the worst thing in the world," said Renata, who had been thinking the whole time. "Sin is the worst thing in the world. Pastor Lopez said it's to blame for all other troubles."

"You're right," said Dad. "Before Adam and Eve sinned, they had no sickness and no trouble. Best of all, they weren't in any trouble with God, so they were always happy. If sin is the *worst trouble,* what is the *best blessing* in the world?"

"I know that too," said Renata. "The forgiveness of sins."

"I'm sure that's right," Dad agreed. "Nothing is more

important than having God's forgiveness and His love. Forgiveness is what removes all our sins. As the Bible tells us, 'In [Jesus] we have ... the forgiveness of sins.' "

Let's talk: What was Renata's question? At first, what did she think the worst thing might be? Why is sin the worst trouble in the world? What is God's best blessing? Why do we have forgiveness all the time? Memorize the Bible verse.

Older children and adults may read: Psalm 130

Let's pray: Dear Father in heaven, we thank and praise You for sending Jesus to save us. Help us believe that "in [Jesus] we have ... the forgiveness of sins." Then we will have the joy of salvation, through Jesus Christ, our Lord. Amen.

Where sin increased, grace increased all the more. Romans 5:20

Always More Love than We Need

It was bedtime, and Mrs. Stevens was up in her daughter Pamela's room for a good-night talk and prayer.

"Mother," said Pamela, "I don't think I can ever be good." She was crying because she had been scolded quite a bit that day.

"You're a good girl now," said Mother. "You're sorry about what you've done wrong."

"But I mean really good, the way God wants me to be," said Pamela.

"Do you think *I'm* that good?" Mother asked.

"Well, maybe" Pamela said, hating to say no. "But I love you anyway because you're good to me."

"Do you think your daddy is as good as God wants him to be?" Mother asked.

"Yes," said Pamela. "Daddy never does anything wrong."

"You ask him," said Mother. "He'll tell you that he does wrong things too, even though he doesn't want to. Is our pastor as good as God wants him to be?"

This time Pamela was very sure. "He must be, or he couldn't be a pastor," she answered.

"But he said last Sunday that he wasn't," Pamela's mother reminded her. "Nobody is as good as God wants him to be. The Bible says there's not a person on earth who does only good and never sins."

"But I do so many wrong things," said Pamela.

"I do many wrong things too," said Mother. "But God loves me just the same, and that's why I love Him. The Bible says, 'Where sin increased, grace increased all the more.' "

"What does that mean?" asked Pamela.

"Let's learn it this way," said Mother. " 'Where sin was great, God's love was much, much greater.' You see, God's love is greater than any sin, and greater than all our sins put together."

"Does that mean God is always willing to forgive us, no matter how much we do wrong?" asked Pamela.

"Yes," said Mother, "that's what's so wonderful about God's love. We're always forgiven because Jesus paid for all our sins. God's love doesn't depend on how good we are."

Let's talk: What worried Pamela? Who did Pamela think was as good as God wants a person to be? What did Mother tell Pamela? Why does God love us even though we often sin? What does the Bible mean when it says, "Where sin increased, grace increased all the more"?

Older children and adults may read: Romans 3:19–24

Let's pray: Dear Father in heaven, we're glad that Your love is greater than all our sins. Please keep on loving us, no matter what. Make us what You want us to be, for Jesus' sake. Amen.

Hallowed be Your name. Matthew 6:9

Honoring God's Holy Name

The O'Connor family was having devotions around the supper table. At the end they all prayed the Lord's Prayer. Even Caitlin, who was only 3 years old, prayed.

When they were finished, her mother said, "Caitlin, tell me how you say the part after 'Our Father who art in heaven.'"

Everybody listened. Caitlin couldn't say her *R*s very well. She said, "Owah Fathah who awt in heaven, Hawold be Thy name."

"I thought that's what you said," Mother said, smiling. "Caitlin, it's not "*Harold.*" It's "*hallowed* be Thy name." Then Mother repeated it a few times until Caitlin said it right.

"What does *hallowed* mean?" asked Brennan, who was 7 years old.

"It means to make something seem holy and great. We pray that God's name will seem great and good to all people," said Mother. "That's because it is holy and great and good."

"God's name is kept holy when people learn the truth about God and live as His children," Father added.

"Tell us in your own words, Dad, what you think when you pray, 'Hallowed be Thy name,'" Mother suggested.

"I might think of it this way," said Dad. "Our Father in heaven, may we do all things in such a way that people will respect Your name and will admire and honor You. Keep me from disgracing Your name, and help me show and teach other people Your love and goodness in sending Jesus to save me."

The last point is especially important. When people

learn how wonderful Jesus is, they begin to love our Father in heaven for sending His Son, Jesus, to save us. And when they love God, then they honor Him and His name.

Let's talk: What were the O'Connors doing around the supper table? What mistake did Caitlin make when she prayed the Lord's Prayer? What does the word *hallowed* mean? Tell in your own words what you mean when you pray, "Hallowed be Thy name." When do people honor and worship God?

Older children and adults may read: Psalm 34:1–10

Let's pray: Holy God, we praise Your name for all Your goodness toward us, especially for Your forgiveness of our sins. Please give us the Holy Spirit so that we will honor You by being good Christians, through Jesus Christ, our Lord. Amen.

We [ought] not rely on ourselves but on God.
2 Corinthians 1:9

Depending on God

It was a cold winter day. The sidewalk was slippery, and in places that weren't shoveled, there was a lot of snow. Sheldon and his father were walking to the store together.

"I don't need you," said young Sheldon when his father tried to hold his hand. "I can walk by myself." But pretty soon he slipped on the ice and started to cry.

"I'll take hold of your coat, Daddy," Sheldon said as they walked on. But in the deep snow he stumbled, and down he went again.

"Daddy, you take my hand," said Sheldon, after he had stopped crying. So his daddy took his hand. When Sheldon slipped again, his daddy held him up and kept him from falling.

"It's better when you hold me than when I hold you," said Sheldon.

"Right," said Daddy. "And it's even better to let God hold us. That's what it means to trust in God. When we trust in God, we let God hold us up and help us."

Even the apostle Paul had to learn this lesson. He got

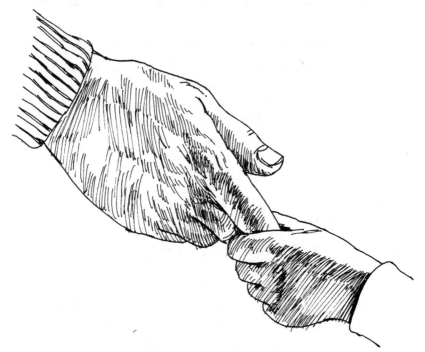

into so much trouble that he thought he would soon be dead. Then he depended on God to help him, and God got him out of his trouble.

Sometimes God lets trouble happen to show us that we don't have a strong hold on Him. When we ask God to take hold of us, things go better. That's how we learn that "we ought not rely on ourselves but on God."

Let's talk: Why did Sheldon keep falling down? When did he not fall anymore? How did the apostle Paul learn to trust God? What does our Bible verse tell us? Why can we trust God and depend on Him?

Older children and adults may read: Psalm 25:1–7

Let's pray: Dear Lord, take my hand and lead me every day. I trust in Your love and power, O Lord. Please keep me from falling into sins and other great troubles. Pick me up when I do fall, for Jesus' sake. Amen.

The LORD is righteous in all His ways and loving toward all He has made. Psalm 145:17

Always Right and Kind

"Mr. Alton died last night," Orah's mother reported at the supper table.

"You mean Craig's daddy?" asked Orah. "I saw him yesterday. He was working in the yard. What happened? Why did he die? He wasn't old and sick."

"Many people die before they get old," Mother answered.

"Didn't God want Mr. Alton to take care of Craig any longer? Who will take care of Craig and his mother? Will she have to get a job?" Orah asked. "Why did God let him die?"

"Now just a minute," Dad said. "Aren't you forgetting something? The Bible says, 'The LORD is righteous in all

His ways and loving toward all He has made.' We don't always know God's reasons, but God must have had a good reason for letting Mr. Alton die. Maybe he was saved from much suffering."

"Maybe he was also kept from losing his faith in Jesus," said Orah's older brother Rafe.

"That would be the best reason God could have for letting someone die," agreed Dad. "People who believe in Jesus never really die. They go on living with God in heaven, where nobody ever dies."

"But what will happen to Craig and his mother?" Orah asked again.

"I'm glad you care," said Mother. "Let's try to find out if we can help them. In the meantime, why don't we ask God to help them too. I'm sure He will."

So they prayed. The next morning Orah's mother went with her to see what they could do for Craig and his mother.

꜅

Let's talk: What may be some of God's reasons for letting people die before they're old? What does the Bible say about everything God does? Where did Craig's father go when he died if he belonged to Jesus? Why is that better than living on earth? Who always takes care of the people who need help on earth?

Older children and adults may read: John 11:20–27

Let's pray: Dear God, our Father in heaven, help us believe that You are right and good in all that You do. When the sadness of death comes, help us think of the blessings that come to Your children through Jesus Christ, our Lord. Give us the Holy Spirit so that we will always trust in Your love, no matter what happens. In Jesus' name we pray. Amen.

The love of money is a root of all kinds of evil.
1 Timothy 6:10

The Love of Money

Cassandra heard about a family that used stories from the newspaper for family devotions. So her dad hung a bulletin board in the kitchen. He told everybody to look for stories to talk about on Friday and to tack them to the board.

The very first week there was a story about a man who killed two people when he robbed a bank. Another story told about two young boys who knocked down an old lady and took her purse. And the church paper reported that someone broke into the Sunday school office and took the mission offering box.

"They all wanted money," said Cassandra when they talked about the stories around the supper table.

"And they all hurt other people to get it," added Devin.

"Why is it always money that makes people do wrong?" asked Cassandra.

"Not quite always," said Mother.

"But look," said Devin, "a man kills two people to get money. Two boys hurt a lady to get her purse. And someone takes the money that was supposed to help our missionaries. Always somebody gets hurt because people love money."

"Don't forget they also hurt themselves and God," said Dad. "Jesus had to suffer and die for the sins of stealing and coveting. His friend Judas even betrayed Him for 30 pieces of silver. It's just as the Bible says, 'The love of money is a root of all kinds of evil.' "

"Is it better to be poor than rich?" asked Devin, a little worried because his father had a good business.

"That depends," said Dad. "It's not the money but the *love* of money that causes the trouble. I hope you'll grow up without loving it. God, in His love, gives you what you need when you need it, and enough to help other people too."

⁓

Let's talk: What kind of devotions did Cassandra's family have on Fridays? What stories were put on the board during the first week? What did all these people try to get? What does the Bible say about the love of money?

Older children and adults may read: 1 Timothy 6:6–11

Let's pray: Thank You, dear Father in heaven, for giving us money to buy the things we need and to do the good You want us to do. Please keep us from loving money and doing wrong to get it. Help us remember that You will give us what You want us to have. In Jesus' name we ask this. Amen.

Love covers over a multitude of sins. 1 Peter 4:8

Why Paul Helped His Sister

"Oh, oh, now there's a big spot on the clean tablecloth," Paul told his sister Ruth. Ruth was setting the table to help her mother, who was at the store. Ruth was not supposed to open the new catsup bottle, but she had, and a big splotch of catsup popped out.

"Please don't tell Mother," said Ruth. "I wanted to surprise her. I'll put on a clean tablecloth and try to wash the spot out later."

"Okay," said Paul. "Let's change it fast. I'll help you."

So Paul and Ruth had the new cloth on the table before their mother came back, and everything looked perfect. "Honey, you're a good little housekeeper," Mother said and kissed Ruth.

When they were alone, Ruth said to Paul, "Thanks for helping me out. I didn't mean to do anything wrong. I'm glad it wasn't noticed."

"It's like the Bible verse we heard Sunday," said Paul.

"Which verse?" asked Ruth.

"Love covers over a multitude of sins," he told her.

"You did cover my sin," said Ruth. "That was Christian love."

"I wouldn't have if you had wanted to do something wrong. But I could see you were sorry," said Paul. "Why don't you tell Mom? She'll understand."

"Guess I will," said Ruth. "Then I'll feel better. And I'm sure she'll forgive me because she loves me just like God does."

Let's talk: What did Ruth do that was wrong? Why was she sorry? How did Paul help Ruth? When might it be wrong to cover up a sin as Paul did? What's another way in which "love covers over a multitude of sins"? Why are Christians willing to forgive other people?

Older children and adults may read: 1 Peter 4:7–10

Let's pray: Dear Lord, we're happy because You forgive the clumsy and wrong things we do. Please make us willing to forgive the sins of others and to help them straighten out what they do wrong. In Jesus' name we ask it. Amen.

The disciples were filled with joy and with the Holy Spirit.
Acts 13:52

Glad to Have Trouble

Did you ever hear of anyone glad to have trouble? The believers in Antioch were. Almost their whole city came to hear Paul and Barnabas preach. But people who hated Jesus made trouble. Paul and Barnabas had to hurry away.

When this happened, did the people who believed in

Jesus worry? No, they didn't. The Bible says, "They were filled with joy and with the Holy Spirit." They were glad that many people were learning about Jesus' love. And they were even willing to be hurt for loving Him.

What makes us glad to have trouble for Jesus? Our love for Him. Grandma Cordell had to work hard to get a big dinner ready whenever her children and grandchildren came to visit. Did she mind? No. Why not? Because she loved them. Love made her glad to have trouble.

Mr. Navarro gave up his fishing trip to get his son from the hospital. Was he sorry to do it? No, he was glad he could. Why? Because he loved his son. Love makes us glad to have trouble.

The new believers in Antioch were glad to have trouble because they loved Jesus. They had just heard how much He had done for them. They were willing to have some trouble for Him too. Instead of being sad or afraid, "they were filled with joy and with the Holy Spirit," says the Bible.

When we remember how Jesus suffered and died for us, and when we love Him as our Savior, then we don't mind any trouble we have because of Him. Instead, it makes us glad.

Let's talk: Why were the believers in Antioch glad when they heard Paul and Barnabas preach? Who made trouble? Why didn't this stop the believers from being glad? What will make us glad to have some trouble for Jesus?

Older children and adults may read: Acts 13:44–52

Let's pray: Dear Lord, our God, please help us understand how much Jesus did for us so that we'll be glad even to have trouble for His sake. Fill us with joy and with the Holy Spirit. We ask this in Jesus' name. Amen.

Let us not become weary in doing good. Galatians 6:9

Piano Practice Can Be Fun

"Guess what!" said Nariko to her friend Gretchen. "I'm starting piano lessons tomorrow. I'm so glad!"

But three months later Nariko said, "Mother, do I *have* to practice piano? I'm tired of it."

"Honey," said Mother, "most things worth learning are hard to do at first. But you mustn't give up so easily. You'll never become a piano player that way."

"But it takes so long to learn," Nariko complained.

"I know," said Mother. "But keep it up, and pretty soon you'll like it. Then you'll be glad you didn't quit when it was hard."

A few weeks later, at the Sunday dinner table, Nariko said, "Being a Christian is like playing the piano, isn't it?"

"In what way is piano playing like being a Christian?" Dad asked.

"Well," said Nariko, "today our pastor told us not to get tired of doing good. 'If you don't quit, someday you'll be glad you didn't,' he said. That's what Mother told me about piano practice."

"I'm sure we all get tired of doing good at times," said Mother. "Yesterday I thought, 'Why do I have to have all the children in the block at my house?' It makes more work for me. I get tired of doing it."

"And I get tired of working at the church," Dad said. "But whenever I do it, I enjoy it. And the more I do for God, the more I enjoy it."

"See what I mean?" said Nariko. "Being a Christian is like playing the piano. The more I practice and the better I play, the more I like it."

"That's why the Bible says, 'Therefore, as we have opportunity, let us do good to all people, especially to those who belong to the family of believers,' " explained Dad. "When we think how much Jesus does for us, it's easy to do good for others."

Let's talk: What did Nariko get tired of doing? What did Mother tell Nariko? What did her pastor preach about? In what way is being a Christian like practicing the piano?

Older children and adults may read: Galatians 6:7–10

Let's pray: Lord Jesus, we're glad that You didn't get tired of saving and helping people. Please keep us from getting tired of doing good for You so that we will be a blessing to others as You are to us. Amen.

Your beauty should not come from [what you wear]. ...
Instead, it should be that of your inner self. 1 Peter 3:3–4

The Best Way to Be Pretty

Meredith and Hadley giggled as they came down the stairs. They were wearing some hats that their mother had worn a long time ago. They also wore some dresses that were much too long and fancy shoes they could hardly keep on their feet.

They giggled still more when they heard their mother coming to see what they were doing. Then they burst out laughing. Mother laughed too. "My, how pretty my girls look today," she said.

"These were pretty clothes long ago, weren't they, Mother?" said Meredith.

"They were my prettiest clothes," Mother told them. "They look funny now because nobody wears that style anymore. Clothes change. But I know a way of dressing up that never changes and never gets old."

"You do?" asked Hadley. She wanted to know all about it.

"Yes, by dressing up on the inside, you'll always be pretty," Mother explained.

"But how can we dress up on the inside?" asked Hadley.

"Well, you see," said Mother, "you are more than just a body. You're also a person living inside your body. The Bible calls this inside person the soul. This part of you, you can dress and decorate by being kind and friendly and sweet and cheerful."

"Jesus gives us those clothes, doesn't He, Mother?" said Meredith, beginning to understand.

"That's right," said Mother. "And God wants everybody to be pretty on the inside. In the Bible, Peter wrote, 'Don't just decorate yourself on the outside, but be pretty on the inside.' "

Meredith looked at her shoes and dress. "Is it wrong to dress up and be pretty on the outside?" she asked.

"No," Mother answered, "it's not wrong, but it's not important. It's much more important to be pretty on the inside because that's what God enjoys seeing."

⌒

Let's talk: What were Meredith and Hadley giggling about? When were those old clothes pretty? Why doesn't that kind of "pretty" stay pretty? In what way does God want us to be pretty? Why is it better to be pretty on the inside? How do we become pretty on the inside?

Older children and adults may read: 1 Peter 3:3–4

Let's pray: Dear God, thank You for making us pretty on the inside by giving us Jesus' love and the Holy Spirit. Teach us to be kind, loving, gentle, and friendly inside, and forgive us when we are mean and selfish and proud. We ask this in the name of Jesus, our beautiful Savior. Amen.

No one can snatch them out of My Father's hand.
John 10:29

Because God Is Holding Us

The wind was blowing hard, and the boat was tipping from side to side. Ray was afraid. He held onto his mother tightly. His father rowed toward the shore as fast as he could. They had been fishing out on the lake when the storm started.

"Mom, I can't hold on any tighter. Don't let me fall out of the boat," cried Ray.

"Don't worry, Ray. I'm holding you," she said.

Ray was holding his mom's arm, but his mom was also holding onto him. And his mom's arms were much stronger than Ray's. So Ray felt safe because his mom held him close.

Some people are afraid they won't be able to hold on to Jesus. Lawrence was afraid. He said, "I told three lies last week, and I argued with my sister. Maybe Jesus won't want me anymore. Maybe I won't get to heaven."

"You can't hold on to Jesus by yourself," his mother said. "But Jesus holds on to you. He promised to do that." This made Lawrence happy.

Jesus said, "No one can snatch you out of My Father's hand." Just as Ray's mother held on to him, so God holds on to us.

⤳

Let's talk: Why was Ray holding on to his mom? Why was Ray safe? Why was Lawrence worried? What did his mother tell him? What did Jesus say in our Bible verse?

Older children and adults may read: John 10:27–30

Let's pray: Dear Father in heaven, we're so glad that You are holding us. Please keep us close to You until we get to live with You in heaven, through Jesus Christ, our Savior. Amen.

Scripture Index